HOPE
IN THE DESERT

HOPE IN THE DESERT

The Churches' United Response to Human Need, 1944-1984

Essays to mark the fortieth anniversary
of the work of the World Council of Churches'
Commission on Inter-Church Aid, Refugee and World Service

Edited by KENNETH SLACK

World Council of Churches, Geneva

Cover design: Michael Dominguez

Cover photo: Peter Williams

ISBN 2–8254–0864–6

© 1986 World Council of Churches, 150 route de Ferney,
1211 Geneva 20, Switzerland

Phototypeset by Input Typesetting Ltd, London
Printed in Switzerland

Behold, I will do a new thing. . .
I will even make a way in the wilderness,
and rivers in the desert.

Isaiah 43:19

Table of contents

Foreword ix Emilio Castro

Editorial Foreword xi

A Note on Terms xv

Inter-Church Aid:
How it all Began 1 Willem A. Visser 't Hooft

A Receiving Church
Becomes a Giving Church 12 Hans Thimme

Inter-Church Aid
and Eastern Europe 30 Ulrich von Brück

Regional Responsibility:
its Joy and Pain 44 Alan A. Brash

Asia 52 Kyaw Than

Africa 63 Samuel H. Amissah

Middle East 71 Archbishop Athanasios

Latin America 78 Marta Palma

Our Ecumenical Diakonia
– Both Large and Small 91 Alexandros Papaderos

Ministering to the Uprooted 107 Kathleen Ptolemy

Inter-Church Aid
and the Future 119 Jean E. Fischer

The Diaconal Task
of the Churches Today 133 Statement by the WCC
Central Committee, Geneva
1984

UNHCR: a Tribute to
Cooperation   136

Directors   141
Contributors   142

Foreword

Here is a book which tells a story of forty years of love in action. It is a story of churches, movements and individuals who have committed themselves to manifest Christian love across frontiers of conflicts and religious, racial and class discrimination. In that sense it is the story of a testimony rendered to Jesus Christ who was rich and became poor so that out of his poverty we all may become rich (2 Cor. 8:9).

It is not a simple success story that is unfolded in these pages. Recognized here is the fact that the struggle to achieve solidarity in service must take into account the imbalances of power and resources among the nations of the world. Temptations of paternalism and dependency are faced honestly. The ambiguities of the human situation which do not allow simple answers or clear-cut solutions are recognized. The polemical, often political, dimensions of Christian service are acknowledged.

The Commission on Inter-Church Aid, Refugee and World Service, whose story is told in this book, belongs to the central concerns of the World Council of Churches' life. It is through this Commission that the churches express their sense of solidarity with one another as they attempt to serve the world. The faithfulness of the service rendered by CICARWS is a measure of the credibility of the ecumenical movement as expressed through the work of the WCC. It is impossible to imagine a WCC without such a means for expressing solidarity, diakonia, care and love.

The book is not meant simply as a celebration of the past. It seeks to face the realities of the present and look to the future. CICARWS is currently going through a phase of self-questioning. It is rethinking its role and redefining its identity, seeking answers to questions like these: What are the services that will faithfully express international Christian solidarity? What kind of an instrument do the churches require in order to render such services?

CICARWS needs to be a forum for theological debates which will examine ways of expressing our belonging to Jesus Christ and our fellowship with humankind. It must examine the meaning and forms of missionary obedience demanded of us today. For this we shall require a process of consultation at national, regional and international levels. That is to say, CICARWS's role cannot be reduced to that of being a mere instrument for effective action. It must generate ideas, and provide for reciprocal inspiration and mutual correction.

CICARWS will need to continue to respond to the world's needs, and to be ready to call for, coordinate, and inspire the responses of the churches. The struggle for human rights, the care of refugees, the response to natural tragedies, the building of the church of Jesus Christ in order to be the servant body of Christ in our nations and countries – these and many other tasks will continue to demand a good deal of time and resources.

Being at the heart of the ecumenical movement, the vocation of CICARWS is also to facilitate the encounter and collaboration of churches and agencies all over the world. No church can be considered to be fully the church of Jesus Christ if it opts out of this mutuality in solidarity. CICARWS does not pretend to be the sole channel through which all expressions of solidarity and co-operation among churches pass, but it is and should remain the defender of the poor, and witness to Jesus Christ in areas of human need.

This book is a celebration of yesterday and an affirmation of our hope for the future. We commend it to readers, and we invite them to join the debate and the service which CICARWS represents.

EMILIO CASTRO
WCC General Secretary

Editorial Foreword

The large-scale, permanent and ecumenical involvement of the churches with world need only began some forty years ago. This book appears to commemorate that striking fact and to give an account, of necessity only partial, of what this involvement has meant.

Of course there is a long tradition of Christian involvement in human need. It goes back to the earliest days of the church's life, to Stephen and his fellow deacons, and to the collection for the needy Christians in Jerusalem which Paul so strenuously advocated. It is a great part of the story of monasticism and very emphatically of the modern missionary movement. Since the ecumenical movement sprang from that missionary movement it is hardly to be wondered at that such service of needy humanity should swiftly become part of its heart. It is still true that the summons of Dr W. A. Visser 't Hooft in 1942 to the Provisional Committee of the World Council of Churches "in process of formation" marked a call to a new dimension of world service. That memorandum is printed in the pages that follow. Prophetically he envisaged that inter-church aid (that is, aid given by the churches acting together and across confessional or denominational boundaries) must be an integral and central part of the new organ of the churches' commitment to unity.

It is interesting nonetheless to observe that his memorandum is headed "Reconstruction of Christian Institutions in Europe". This was the immediate task. You could say that the story of the succeeding four decades of this work, reflected in these pages, is the story of every boundary or limitation, whether of space or time, being swept away as the Spirit has moved the churches to a response that is permanent, comprehensive and worldwide.

This is not only shown in the essays which follow those devoted to the German scene – essays that deal with the regionalizing of the work, and with aspects of it in Asia, Africa, the Middle East and Latin America – but in the constant revelation in these pages that the demands of human need cannot be limited. They cannot be limited to the aftermath of war, or the impact of natural catastrophe. The millions of those whose plight never reaches the headlines, who do not become refugees because of political upheaval, or face homelessness because of flood or earthquake, but who are born into a cycle of deprivation have an equal claim on Christian compassion. Not the victims of specific events but the victims of an unjust world call for solidarity. They are born into malnutrition, inadequate shelter and the absence of health care. The test of the depth of this new movement for Christian response to world need has been whether the churches could go on caring when the emergency is no longer floodlit by media concern. But it has even more been whether that caring could be deep enough and sustained enough to comprehend the full scale of world poverty.

Increasingly, too, the movement has been tested by the issue of whether it was willing to add to the concern to give specific help to victims a commitment to working for those basic changes in our world which will reduce the number of such victims. This is at the heart of the profound essay contributed to this symposium by Alexandros Papaderos in which he draws the distinction between "microdiakonia" and "macrodiakonia". It may be added that it is growing commitment to the latter which inevitably brings with it controversy. In fact the deeper the commitment has become across the past forty years to an inter-church aid which is prophetic rather than simply philanthropic, the more the work is attended by controversy. But this has been the lot of the ecumenical movement as a whole.

This finds particular reflection in the contribution on Latin America made by Marta Palma. Concern for the physical wellbeing of victims cannot exhaust true Christian concern. It must inevitably be matched by concern for human rights. Such concern of necessity has political implications. Constantly the years have tested the reality of the ecumenical commitment to offer help in Christ's name to those who suffer, regardless of colour, creed or political conviction. In earlier years it might be said that the test was not a severe one: the great mass of those who were helped did not possess convictions which disturbed the donors. Many, for example, were refugees from communism, and this commended them to many donors in the West. In more recent years those who have fled from racist regimes or right-wing tyrannies have raised other questions. It has been something of a glory of the work of Inter-Church Aid that it has honoured its universal and undiscriminating mandate as controversy – often fomented by opponents of the ecumenical ideal – has mounted.

That ecumenical channels have not always been chosen either by recipients or donors is honestly faced in some of the essays which follow. That we are still a good way from emerging from that recipient/donor relationship is also admitted. As I have edited this book I have been glad that there has been such honesty in the writing, and at times an astringently critical look at some attitudes and issues (Alan Brash's article on regionalization is an example). But the effect of reading the book as a whole is refreshingly encouraging to faith and church involvement today.

What is portrayed here is really a new dimension of discipleship – the calling of God's Spirit to Christians of very many traditions to permanent engagement at every level with human need, and above all commitment to need that is not on their doorstep but right across the world. Without this commitment the movement for unity would have become introverted; with it, the movement becomes demandingly and enrichingly relevant to a world made technologically one while remaining dangerously morally divided.

That the obedience to the calling of the Spirit has been only partial and inadequate is acknowledged. That there *has* been such obedience and that it has borne so much fruit is a source of deep thanksgiving. "This is the Lord's doing, and it is marvellous in our eyes."

Kenneth Slack
Editor

Note
I am grateful to the Language Service of the World Council for much help in the preparation of the material. And I owe and express particular thanks to two old colleagues and friends for much help: Shelagh Friedli, my essential contact in Geneva, and Anne Borthwick who, once again, has produced a fine typescript from somewhat intractable material for a book in which I was engaged.

A Note on Terms

I have not thought it necessary to be pedantic over the terms used to describe the united work of the churches in meeting human need in the essays which follow. Historical accuracy would have required careful amendment to precise descriptions in use at the time that the author was describing. Again, sometimes CICARWS, that is, the Commission on Inter-Church Aid, Refugee and World Service, is used, and sometimes DICARWS, the Division of Inter-Church Aid, Refugee and World Service – the name of the department prior to WCC restructuring in 1971. "The Commission" is the name given to the committee which oversees the work of CICARWS.

The words "inter-church aid" are sometimes used with a precise meaning of church to church help, chiefly across confessional boundaries, but most often they are used to describe the whole work of the World Council of Churches in the field of the Commission, including therefore refugee work and development. The words "inter-church aid" then refer to the ecumenical nature of the enterprise.

Care has only been taken to avoid confusion by the variety of terms.

Editor

Inter-Church Aid: How it all Began

Willem A. Visser 't Hooft

The following is the key "foundation document" of inter-church aid in the life of the World Council of Churches – the memorandum submitted by Dr Willem Visser 't Hooft to the Provisional Committee of the World Council of Churches "in process of formation". It is followed by a brief reflection on what happened, and what followed, which Dr Visser 't Hooft wrote in December 1984, a few months before his death.

★ ★ ★ ●

I. RECONSTRUCTION OF CHRISTIAN INSTITUTIONS IN EUROPE

The following memorandum has been submitted to a meeting of members of the Provisional Committee at Geneva on Friday, 25 September 1942, and has been accepted by them as a statement of their common view concerning the task of reconstruction to be accomplished in Europe after the war and the best means of accomplishing this task.

1. Introduction

Although many churches are at present unable to formulate their needs and to communicate these to their sister churches, there is already a strong desire in several churches (e.g. in the United States, Great Britain, Switzerland, and Sweden) to begin to prepare for the task of post-war reconstruction. This memorandum represents an attempt to describe one segment of the task which will in all likelihood have to be performed. Its purpose is not to discuss the reconstruction task in general, and it speaks, therefore, not of such important Christian tasks as those of peace-making and reconciliation between the nations. Nor does it speak of the aid which will have to be given to churches in Asia and Africa. Its purpose is merely to state what the churches included in the ecumenical movement can and should do to help those many Protestant, Eastern Orthodox, and Old Catholic churches and

Christian bodies on the European continent which will badly need help. It is hoped that similar memoranda will be worked out for other areas where there exist similar needs.

2. The need

The full extent of the need will only become manifest at the end of the war, but it is already clear that the task of reconstruction will be immense and will demand the concerted action of all churches and Christian organizations. It would seem that the main relief tasks will be the following:

a) Restoration of ruined churches and other buildings such as parish houses, Christian schools, hospitals, etc. The number of cities where all or many church buildings have been ruined is constantly increasing.

b) The furnishing of funds to those churches which have been wholly or largely disorganized and whose funds have been confiscated. It is unlikely that the new post-war governments will be able to repay to these churches the funds which they have lost and which they will need to rebuild their church organization.

c) The reconstitution of the Christian organizations and movements which have been forbidden and which have in many cases lost all their funds and reserves. This is especially necessary in the realm of youth work. Much will depend for the future of the church in Europe on the possibility to reconstruct the Christian youth movement on the strongest possible basis.

d) To provide the churches and Christian movements with the pastors and lay workers whom they need. In several countries the number of pastors is rapidly decreasing and the processes of recruiting and training for the ministry have almost wholly stopped. There will be the need of temporary help for certain countries by other countries in men, in scholarships, in funds for the training of ministers and lay workers, in subsidies to theological seminaries, etc.

e) To enable Christian relief organizations, such as the home mission bodies and other Christian institutions for the poor, the sick, the orphans, the refugees, etc. not only to continue their work, but also to widen its scope in view of the enormous need for physical and medical relief which will exist after the war.

f) To help in the production of Christian literature. In many countries the publication of Christian literature has almost wholly ceased and the available stocks have been sold out. There is already a very great demand for Bibles, simple commentaries, evangelistic literature, and theological works.

g) The re-establishment of the missionary boards in countries where the home base of the foreign missionary work has been disorganized. While the great service of solidarity organized for the "orphaned missions", which may well have to be continued for a time after the war, belongs rather under the heading "reconstruction work in Asia and Africa", the help to be given to the mission boards in Europe so as to enable them to take over again their full share of the missionary task is an integral part of the task of Christian reconstruction in Europe.

3. Changes in European church life which have to be specially kept in mind

Owing to the totalitarian character of this war, the churches have been immeasurably more deeply involved in and affected by this war than by previous wars. The main effects of this situation which have a bearing on reconstruction work are:

a) A number of churches have gone or are going through church conflicts of such a radical character that their structure of organization is almost wholly disrupted. It will take many years of peace before these churches will have reorganized themselves. This means that in a number of countries the channels through which relief should normally be given will not exist in the first period after the war, and that the first task of reconstruction in these countries will be to assist in the rebuilding of the whole church organization.

b) The suffering, very particularly the spiritual suffering, in the European countries results in deep transformations in faith and attitude, which create a gulf between those who have gone through that experience and those who have not. Even those who belong to these countries themselves, but who have been forced to emigrate, can only very partly understand what is going on in the hearts and minds of their countrymen. An immense effort of spiritual imagination is needed on the part of those who would help the Christians of these countries.

c) At the same time the churches of many countries have through these years of conflict developed a much stronger sense of their responsibility to the nation as a whole; they have accordingly come to occupy a far more central place in the life of their respective nations and their tasks and opportunities in relation to the spiritual, social, and political reconstruction will, therefore, be far more considerable than they were after the last war. They must be helped to perform these new nationwide tasks and to take advantage of these increased opportunities.

d) Thus the churches will have new tasks in relation to the masses of the workers. The wall of separation between the church and the working class is being broken down and new opportunities for large-scale evangelization and Christian social work are emerging on all sides.

e) Similarly the youth problem will take on tremendous proportions. Youth in many countries is uprooted and demoralized. Governments will have to take a far larger share in the formation of youth than before, but since the basic problem to be faced is a spiritual problem, the churches will have to bear a very large part of the total burden.

f) The new church consciousness which has arisen through these years of conflict has the effect that the churches desire to carry much larger responsibility in the realm of evangelism, social work, youth work, etc. than they did before. It will be necessary to enable the churches to fulfill this responsibility, but it will also be necessary to make sure that this new church-centred conception of Christian work does not lead to the suppression of lay movements and lay activity.

g) The deep hatred which has arisen in the hearts of the oppressed peoples will make collaboration even between Christians of countries who have fought against each other (sometimes also those of one and the same country) very difficult and will have an important bearing on the willingness to give for particular countries, and the willingness to send workers to particular areas.

h) At the same time, it can be said that there is also among Christian leaders a very real sense of ecumenical solidarity. This is as yet confined to those who have had an opportunity to be directly or indirectly associated with the ecumenical movement. It will, therefore, be necessary in the years after the war to intensify and strengthen the work of the ecumenical movement and to make sure that through large-scale conferences, such as the Amsterdam conference, through training institutes, and through ecumenical literature the reality of the church universal is brought home to the individual members of the churches.

4. The spirit which is needed

a) In order that the reconstruction work may truly build the church, and that both in the sense of restoration of Christian institutions and in the sense of the manifestation of the church universal, it must be undertaken in the spirit of Christian koinonia, that is in the spirit of solidarity, of unselfish and unconditional sharing between those who recognize each other as members of one and the same body of Christ.

b) This means that the service to be rendered is to be rendered in a truly ecumenical manner, so that all churches which can help come to the rescue of all churches which need help. This does not exclude the possibility of the establishment of special relationships between churches of one and the same confession, but it does exclude competition between the churches, and the use of relief money to carry on proselytism among Christians of another denomination. It should, for instance, be very clearly stated that Protestant churches which accept relief tasks in Eastern Orthodox countries will not use their presence for purposes of proselytism. An ecumenical service does imply that each church agrees to work through and with the churches which exist in each given country, and accepts to have its reconstruction work coordinated with the reconstruction work of other churches.

c) It means also that the help to be given should be given in a spirit which transcends all national idiosyncrasies. All countries which can help are to help all the countries which need help. And the supranational character of the help given should become manifest through the coordination of all Christian reconstruction work by an ecumenical international body. Only thus can a reaction against real or supposed spiritual imperialism of a nation or a group of nations be avoided.

d) For the same reasons the action of the churches should be an independent action which is neither in organization, nor in spirit depending upon governmental relief projects. Governments will have to take considerable initiative with regard to relief in the post-war era. But their activities will inevitably be set in the framework of the political aspirations which they desire to realize and will, therefore, call forth political reactions. The relief work of the churches should move in a higher realm, and this must become clear in that it is seen to be motivated solely by Christian solidarity.

5. The men who will be needed

Many churches in need will be unable to carry out the reconstruction task unless Christian workers from other churches come to assist them in the organization of reconstruction. Moreover, a considerable part of the task will consist in the providing of church workers from other countries for those where the ranks of pastors and lay workers have been depleted. It will, therefore, be necessary to arrange for an ecumenical and international sharing of resources in men, such as has taken place in relation to Asia and Africa through the missionary movement, but never on a large scale in relation to Europe.

The European countries themselves can provide a not unconsiderable number of the workers' needs, for there are countries (e.g. Sweden and Switzerland) which have at present a larger number of theological students than they need for their own immediate tasks. But in view of the magnitude of the task, this inter-European sharing will not suffice and there will, therefore, be a need for workers from overseas.

Much will depend on the choice of these workers. The qualities which are needed above all are definite Christian conviction and spiritual imagination. The European churches having gone through a time of trial, such as they have not known since the Reformation, are turning back to the foundations of their faith in the Bible, and those who would help them must take their stand with them on the foundation which has made it possible to these churches to remain firm in the midst of the onslaught upon them. And spiritual imagination will be needed in order to understand what has gone on in the hearts and minds of European Christians during the years of suffering.

Special qualities are required in cases where workers of one confession will have to work among those of another confession (very especially in the case of Protestants working among the Eastern Orthodox). No one should be allowed to go and work in and for another confessional situation without having previously acquainted himself with the tenets and spirit of the church to which he is sent.

It might be possible to work out a plan according to which the choice of personnel for each country and church could be made by representatives of the sending and the receiving church together so that maladjustments and disappointments may be avoided.

It is not too early to start preparing men for these tasks. Language courses and courses in modern history will be essential for those who would come over. But even more important would be courses of "ecumenics" which help the candidates for work overseas to get a living picture of the faith, life, and work of the churches which they may have to assist. Here lies a great task for the theological colleges and faculties.

6. The money which will be needed

It is at present impossible to estimate the resources which will be needed. A number of continental churches are at present in a relatively favourable financial condition, but this is due to circumstances which will certainly not last, and which are likely to be followed by a period of general impoverishment. One of these circumstances is that the opportunities to use their income are so very restricted (no opportunity for building or reparation, for the production of literature, fewer pastors, no expenses for missionary work, etc.). Another one is that in present circumstances money has lost its buying value and is, therefore, more easily given away, especially to the few causes which still remain of the many to which money used to be contributed. It is, however, likely that larger gifts will no longer be available just at the moment when they will be most needed. Thus it will undoubtedly be necessary to mobilize all resources of all churches in order to meet the main needs which have arisen already and which will yet arise.

7. The organization which will be needed

The task to be accomplished is so great that no church body, no single confession, and no single group of churches of one nation can possibly perform it alone. The reconstruction work will, therefore, have to be done by many churches of different nations for many churches of different nations. Thus the problem of coordination becomes acute. Unless organs of consultation and coordination can be established, there is real danger that there will be much overlapping in different fields or considerable conflict in policy, and that important areas of need will be forgotten.

Now the vast majority of churches which will either give or receive help have already collaborated in the ecumenical movement, and have accepted membership in the World Council of Churches. In fact, the World Council is the only body in which practically all these churches are represented *as churches*. By putting the whole work in the setting of the fellowship of the World Council it will be possible to arrive at a voluntary coordination which leaves every church free to act within the framework of a generally accepted policy. Thus also it will be possible to avoid the impression that any church or national group tries to dominate others. What is needed is, therefore, the creation of a reconstruction department of the World Council with a committee widely representative of both giving and receiving churches.

It is suggested that the Reconstruction Department of the World Council should take over the work of the European Central Bureau for Inter-Church Aid, which was founded in 1922, and which has rendered such great services in meeting the needs of the churches in the difficult period after the last war and the succeeding period. The tradition and experience of the Central Bureau will be of great value in the building up of the new organization which is now needed to meet the even greater needs of the present day and which must be adapted to the new situation and possibilities of the ecumenical movement due to the coming into existence of the World Council of Churches.

The functions of the new department may be described as follows:

a) to survey the needs of all churches and Christian organizations which are members of or collaborate with the ecumenical movement;

b) to bring these needs to the attention of the churches which are able to give help;

c) to register all projects of aid from one church to another, and to coordinate these projects;

d) to formulate and develop relief projects in cases in which the help of several churches is needed;

e) to act as an executive agency of relief itself in cases in which it is asked to do so by one or more giving churches.

It goes without saying that the officers of the committee should represent different confessions and different nations, and that an equally ecumenical and international group of staff workers should be chosen.

8. First steps to be taken

In order that the reconstruction work may be started immediately after the war, it is necessary to begin preparations at once. For the present these preparations should be in the hands of the general secretaries of the Provisional Committee under the guidance of the chairman of the Administrative Committee and in consultation with the church leaders of as many countries as possible. But as soon as possible after the war a special committee for this purpose should be appointed.

It will be advisable to choose as soon as possible a person who can give full time to these preparations. The American churches would render a signal service to the ecumenical cause if they would make available, at least for a limited period, one of their leaders to the Geneva staff of the World Council for this difficult work of preparation, and thus ensure that from the very beginning there will be the closest possible collaboration in this whole realm between the American and the European churches. Since there is at the moment no American on the Geneva staff of the World Council, such an appointment would not only be of great value in preparing for the post-war era, but also in relation to the immediate tasks.

It is also desirable that some of the main churches or families of churches in the countries which are most able to help should assign their own representatives to cooperate in the general plan of reconstruction, such representatives being supported by their own churches and being accredited to the World Council of Churches for the working out of the coordinated programme and participation in it.

II. FORTY YEARS ON

When, at the meeting in 1938 called to draw up a constitution for the World Council of Churches, the representatives of the churches defined that council as "a fellowship of churches", they became inevitably committed to the working out of a structure of relations between the churches in which inter-church aid would have a very important place. For in the language of the Christian church, that word "fellowship" (koinonia) is a most substantial expression describing the life of the church as the common life of a people who, because of their sharing in the confession of one and the same Lord, are expected to share the spiritual and material gifts which they have received. St Paul teaches that "the gracious work" of practising solidarity belongs to the essence of the new life and is a test of its reality (2 Cor. 8–9).

In those years before the Second World War, the two main branches of the ecumenical movement Life and Work and Faith and Order did not include inter-church aid among their activities. There was another organization: the European Central Bureau for Inter-Church Aid, directed by Dr Adolf Keller, which did useful work, but was not sufficiently rooted in the life of the churches and had no clearly defined relation with other parts of the ecumenical movement. What was needed was a system of mutual aid for which all the churches would feel responsible and which would have its rightful place in the total life of the ecumenical movement. When I was asked whether I would consider a call to become general secretary of the new World Council, I wrote to Dr J. H. Oldham (in 1937) that among the conditions which I would make would be the readiness of the council to become active in the field of mutual aid, for there could be no healthy ecumenical fellowship without practical solidarity.

The war years made the problem of inter-church aid vastly more urgent and acute. We began, therefore, to prepare for the enormous post-war tasks. What form should the enterprise take? The basic principle was clear: all churches which were able to help should come to the rescue of the churches which needed help. That did not mean the ignoring of confessional ties but transcending them sufficiently so that (as St Paul had put it) none received too little and none received too much. For this purpose coordination was required and this could be done by forming in both giving and receiving countries national inter-church aid committees or agencies which would inform the churches about the needs to be met, establish contacts between needy churches which were not in touch with giving churches and churches able to help and under-take common activities for all the needy churches in a given area. These plans were discussed with representatives of the American and Swiss churches in 1942 when Dr S. McCrea Cavert came to Geneva, and in 1944, when Dr A. L. Warnshuis did the same. So, at the end of the war, the new Department of Reconstruction and Inter-Church Aid could begin to function. Its first director was Dr J. H. Cockburn, a former moderator of the General Assembly of the Church of Scotland. The American churches sent a number of representatives to help in creating an adequate staff at headquarters in Geneva.

In the following years, the task became enlarged in three ways. In view of the need of food and clothing in several parts of Europe, material aid for needy people inside or outside the churches became necessary. The department became a tool of the churches for emergency aid. Secondly, the department began to be concerned with Asia, Africa and Latin America. The needs of the younger churches had been cared for by the International Missionary Council with its orphaned missions programme. Gradually the World Council of Churches began to participate in meeting the needs of these continents. Thirdly, the service to refugees which had begun in the days of the Nazi persecution of the Jews, but which had now to cope with very large groups of refugees from Eastern Europe, became part of the department.

I wrote forty years ago that the way the churches would act in this field would become the test of the reality of the ecumenical movement. "If it proves possible to act in a truly brotherly fashion in this realm, the ecumenical movement will be shown to exist as a living organism. If, however, denominational and confessional individualism triumphs, the ecumenical movement will be shown to be a matter of theory."

Was that not expecting too much from churches which had not learned to cooperate and to conceive the task of the church in ecumenical terms? It was. The picture of Inter-Church Aid in the post-war era was not that of a perfectly coordinated operation in which all participating churches accepted the guidance of ecumenical bodies. But we can fortunately add that the majority of the churches did enter into the proposed ecumenical system to a greater or lesser extent. With few exceptions, the member churches of the World Council who could help spent at least part of their aid on churches which did not belong to their confessional family.

It seems to me that as we look back on the history of the ecumenical movement during the last forty years, we can make the following affirmations about the significance which Inter-Church Aid, Refugee and World Service has had in the life of the movement. The churches have begun to learn the lesson of the coherence of the body of Christ. As one member suffers, all suffer. So, Inter-Church Aid, not only across national frontiers, but also across confessional frontiers, has become in many churches an accepted practice. The churches have learned to undertake significant practical common tasks: health programmes, scholarships, service to refugees, work camps for youth, ecumenical loan fund, etc. And they have accepted responsibility for common action in meeting the need for material aid in situations when people anywhere in the world suffer as a result of natural disasters. Finally, for many men and women – both those on the giving and those on the receiving side – inter-church aid was the only form of concrete and personal participation in the ecumenical movement, and it made them aware that the *familia Dei* is not just a beautiful dream.

A Receiving Church
Becomes a Giving Church

Hans Thimme

Dr Hans Thimme in the article which follows reflects on some forty years of involvement in Inter-Church Aid, especially from the viewpoint of a German churchman. In 1945 he was one of many in his land who looked to Inter-Church Aid for succour. Later the church in West Germany became one of the greatest contributors to Inter-Church Aid, and he was for seven years moderator of DICARWS.

★ ★ ★

A personal note

When I set off to attend the Fourth Assembly of the World Council of Churches at Uppsala in 1968 it was with the firm resolve not to accept any new ecumenical office. I had been a member of various WCC departments since 1954 and wanted now to give more time, and even to devote myself exclusively, to my increasingly heavy and numerous official responsibilities in my own church. But things were to turn out otherwise. When asked to work with the Division of Inter-Church Aid I felt I had no right to refuse. To be sure, I was no expert in "service" matters, nor did I represent officially any of the church aid agencies. I had begun my service in the church as a pastor of a local congregation and basically that was what I still remained. Even in my later episcopal responsibility my main interest remained evangelism and mission and the question of the ways and means whereby the church is to do justice to its missionary calling. But the DICARWS invitation touched a deep chord in my heart.

In the first years after the Second World War, both personally and as representative of my regional church in Germany, I had had firsthand experience of DICARWS aid. It was to DICARWS that I owed the fresh start in my life as a pastor at that time, and what ecumenical aid had done for the reconstruction of church and society in post-war Germany remained indelibly printed on my mind. As one who had been a recipient of DICARWS aid, I was sure that I had no right now to turn a deaf ear to the invitation to help directly in its own work. And so I became moderator of DICARWS for the period between the Uppsala (1968) and Nairobi (1975) Assemblies of the World Council of Churches. During that time I used every opportunity in private and in public to emphasize the indissoluble connection between giving and receiving in inter-church aid. In reality, the distinction between donor churches and recipient churches is quite spurious. Not simply because, as I know from my own experience, a receiving church can very quickly become a giving church, but also because giving can be at the same time an integral part of its receiving and receiving an integral part of its giving. This complementarity of giving and receiving is the real secret of the koinonia in the worldwide community of Jesus Christ. If, in what follows, I simply tell of my own experiences in Germany from 1945 onwards, I am doing no more than reporting some basic insights which have influenced me in my work in DICARWS, as in my life in the church generally.

How it began

In a Germany completely isolated and sealed off by the war, we were quite unaware that as early as 1942 ideas about how to help post-war reconstruction of the churches in Europe, and even in Germany, were already circulating in the ecumenical movement. We were thrown back on ourselves and increasingly despairing of ourselves as time went on. The really appalling thing when the war ended was not just the millions of the dead, soldiers and civilians, not just the houses destroyed in cities and countryside, not just the complete collapse of all productive social and economic life, nor simply the conditions of terrible material distress; the really appalling thing was the mood of profound discouragement and despair which had bitten deep into the souls of our people. Guilt and fatalism in like measure led to a hopeless sense of utter repudiation and abandonment. In such circumstances how could there possibly be a fresh start at all? On what basis and by what means? Material aid, however vitally needed, could not really be the decisive step. There was understandable reticence towards it on both sides at first. It was along the spiritual road that the real breakthrough came. A new spiritual beginning laid the foundations for practical ecumenical cooperation which very quickly broadened out until it eventually embraced all areas of life.

In October 1945, an ecumenical delegation came to Stuttgart on its own initiative. Besides Dr W. A. Visser 't Hooft it included Dr Samuel McCrea Cavert of the National Council of Churches of the USA, Dr S. C. Michelfelder of the Lutheran Church of

America, Bishop George Bell of Chichester, Pastor Pierre Maury of France, Dr Hendrik Kraemer of the Netherlands, and Dr Adolf Koechlin of Switzerland. Their purpose was to conduct preliminary discussions with representatives of the Evangelical Churches in Germany. The visit took place at a time when the occupation forces were strictly forbidden to "fraternize" with the German population. The German people and the Christian family in Germany, too, were overcome by a sense of guilt and shame, embarrassment and apathy. The very fact that the oikoumene outside Germany should in these circumstances have taken the first step to re-establish contact was in itself inter-church aid of the kind that matters most. Visser 't Hooft recalls how deeply moved he was by Martin Niemöller's sermon in Stuttgart on the passage in Jeremiah (Jer. 14:7–11) which begins "Though our iniquities testify against us, act, O Lord, for Thy Name's sake". Then came the Stuttgart Declaration of Guilt, so basic for the new church beginning in Germany, read out by Bishop Wurm of Württemberg on behalf of the Council of the Evangelical Church in Germany:

> It is with deep pain that we acknowledge that through us untold suffering has been visited on many peoples and lands. On behalf of the whole church we now declare publicly what we often testified to our congregations: Although we have, in the name of Jesus Christ, struggled for many years against the spirit which found frightful embodiment in the National Socialist tyranny, we blame ourselves for having failed to bear more courageous testimony, to pray more faithfully, to believe more joyfully, to love more ardently. A fresh start must now be made in our churches. . . . It fills us with profound joy to know that, in this new beginning, we are truly one with the other churches of the ecumenical fellowship. Before God, we hope that, in the common service of the churches, the spirit of violence and revenge which seeks to renew its force today may be checked throughout the world and that the spirit of peace and love whereby tortured humanity may alone find healing may prevail.

How the ecumenical guests responded to this declaration is described by Visser 't Hooft in his memoirs:

> Pastor Pierre Maury was the first to respond. He said that the ecumenical delegation welcomed the declaration without any sense of moral superiority. These words would help the other churches in their struggle for justice. Their response would not be: "At last the Germans have repented." They would regard the German declaration as a summons to renew their own Christian life and to fulfill the common task of reconverting Europe to the Christian faith. Bishop Bell said that in common fidelity to Christ the churches wanted to work from now on together for a just and peaceful order. I myself added that it

was the duty of the other churches and of the World Council itself to ensure that the declaration was not exploited for political ends.

It was here, then, that inter-church aid really began in Germany after 1945. Here the foundations were laid for the way forward – penitence and pardon were the basis on which constructive work in freedom and frankness became possible. There were now no longer any inhibitions preventing giving and receiving. Christian solidarity apparently rests on a deeper foundation than just compassion and sympathy.

An Evangelical country parson after 1945

When I returned to my Westphalian parish of Spenge in the summer of 1945, after five years of military service and a short period as a prisoner of war in American hands, I experienced in a very personal way what had taken place in Stuttgart representatively for the whole of the Evangelical Church in Germany. This was how it came about. The headquarters of the British Army of Occupation was located in Bünde, not far from Spenge. Attached to it was the Division for Church Affairs, with the Rev. Frank de Jonge, the Rev. Edwin Robertson and the Rev. Ian Wilson, who also worked closely with the Geneva Department of Church Reconstruction in Europe. What were my experiences of inter-church aid from this quarter?

Because of its remoteness, Spenge had remained almost untouched by aerial bombing. But apart from the few farmers in the congregation, most of our members lacked just about everything. The average daily food ration was at most 1,500 calories. Clothes were down to the last few pitiful remnants. In addition to this, a large number of refugees who had fled from the bombing in the Ruhrland, which was a part of our Westphalian Church, were billeted in the homes of members of our congregation. There was also a constant stream of refugees from the eastern zones of Germany. In the end the parish population had grown from an initial 7,000 to 10,500. In my vicarage, for example, where before the war I had lived alone with my family, there were in 1946 not only an additional trio of bombed-out relatives but also three other families, a total of twenty-four people.

In such a situation, what could be done? Many forms of self-help developed quite spontaneously. In many cases, the result of the general scarcity was a great willingness to share what was to hand. Very soon, too, American CARE parcels started to arrive in increasing numbers as well as ecumenical gifts from Britain, Holland and Switzerland. I shall have more to say about this later.

But what was Frank de Jonge up to in nearby Bünde? From the outside it appeared only very little. Yet he clearly had an amazing flair for winkling out pastors and church members whose names had been supplied to him by the Confessing Church and whom he considered to be potential bridge-builders and effective multipliers. Eventually he gathered around him men like Ernst Wilm, Klaus von Bismarck, Hans Heinrich Harms, Hans Heinrich Wolf, Heinrich Puffert, Hans Lilje, Wilhelm Hahn – and myself. All of us were subsequently to become active in a wide variety of fields. Since at first we hardly knew each other, how he managed to find us remains a mystery to me. He visited our homes and introduced us to one another. He invited us to Bünde for cocktail parties (a style of male conviviality which seemed at first more than a little strange to a simple country pastor, especially in the early post-war months, though it certainly proved an effective way of establishing confidence!). In all this he was simply demonstrating in practical ways a Christian solidarity and friendship which bridged the frontiers and the gaping chasms. A few months later we had another practical example of his friendship when we were invited to join a Christian retreat in a home for British officers. When we found ourselves being served there with an early morning cup of tea in bed by a British soldier in uniform at 7 o'clock each morning – a quite unusual luxury – the effect on us was overwhelming. We were equally moved by the communion service in the chapel.

In the following year – 1946 – we were invited to spend several weeks in England to make contacts: a week in an Anglican country vicarage near Oxford, and a week in the Wistow guest house near Sheffield presided over with loving care by an emigrant German couple. This made an indelible impression on us. Since my scholar-ship year in Princeton, New Jersey, in the USA in 1932–33, I had never been outside Germany, nor had I been able to maintain contacts by correspondence. Now I was once again accepted completely as a member of the ecumenical family. During the week in the Anglican vicarage I had the privilege of reading the daily responses with the vicar in the otherwise empty church. In Wistow there were many opportunities for reflection on our burdened German past. I returned from England permanently enriched. What then was Frank de Jonge's way of practising inter-church aid? Apart from the cocktails, and perhaps, too, the 100 grams of coffee for my wife, the decisive thing was achieved through the direct personal affirmation of community, spiritual sustenance and comfort, the encouragement to make a fresh start. This creative stimulus soon produced its effect. Material aid was not the primary and decisive thing. Nor were Frank de Jonge and

Edwin Robertson the only ones to help and encourage us. I shall never forget Hebe Kohlbrügge either. She was a Dutch resistance fighter recently released from a German concentration camp, who now spent her time travelling from one Evangelical vicarage to another, radiating forgiveness, love, encouragement and trust. At the same time she demonstrated in a very practical way the direction to take if spiritual and material reconstruction was to succeed. Mention must also be made of Janet Lacey who (later burdened with the enormous task of organizing Christian Aid) by her shining personal devotion showed that encouragement and inspiration was more important than any material aid.

The situation in the congregations at that time

My own congregation of Spenge belonged to the Evangelical Church of Westphalia which, with its more than three million members, was one of the largest of the regional churches in the German Evangelical Church. The destruction wrought by the war is difficult for us to imagine today: 330 of the 610 churches, 236 of the 249 parish buildings, 28 of the 35 hospitals, 85 of the 118 infant-schools, 363 of the 692 vicarages, were either completely destroyed or seriously damaged; 51 Westphalian pastors, 68 assistant pastors, 26 probationer pastors and 15 theological students had been killed, while 16 pastors, 18 assistant pastors and one probationer pastor were missing; 28,065 people had been killed in the bombing raids. The parishes mourned 96,732 war dead and 185,686 missing. From the eastern zones and Czechoslovakia at the end of the war, over twelve million expelled Germans streamed into the ruins and devastation of western Germany with its desperate and discouraged population; 1.4 million of these refugees (half of them Evangelicals) came to Westphalia. In finding emergency accommodation for these people, no account could be taken of their religion, of course, and so it came about that regions of Westphalia which had previously been almost exclusively Evangelical now had to cope with a sizeable minority of Catholics, and vice versa. The old sixteenth century rule of *cuius regio, eius religio* (the religion of a region is that of its ruler) no longer applied. From now on, the resultant mixture of the Christian confessions imposed the additional difficulty of ensuring that hundreds of thousands of church members in the newly created diaspora were provided with appropriate pastoral care. Churches had to be built and pastors appointed – an utterly impossible task!

The general situation at that time has been described as follows by Herbert Grundmann in his *Handbook of German History*:

In many cases people became apathetic. Any vital energy they still had left was used up in the struggle to survive. But mutual aid was also initiated and organized civic efforts begun. In the towns a start was made on clearing away the mountains of rubble by civilian labour. Local authorities freshly organized by the military governments began their work. Slowly the destroyed and damaged hospitals and then the schools and colleges were rehabilitated. . . . Private and commercial traffic had virtually vanished from the streets. . . . Rail traffic was only slowly resumed, since tracks had been destroyed and there was a shortage of locomotives and wagons. In the few crowded trains – unheated even in winter – people stood tightly packed together, clutching their bundles, seeking their homes or some new abode, or undertaking long trips to the countryside or the coast to find food somewhere or other. Without the help from abroad, the supply situation would have been worse still. In the British and American zones, even the smallest rations were only possible because certain foodstuffs were imported at the expense of the occupying power. In addition there was considerable voluntary aid from many neutral countries and even from formerly enemy countries. Food parcels were sent from Britain even though rationing was still in force there for some years after the end of the war. Welfare organizations in the United States set up the mammoth CARE programme for the despatch of voluntary aid to distressed countries.

The creation of the Evangelical Relief Agency in Germany

As we have heard, thinking about post-war reconstruction had already begun in Geneva during the war; there Dr Hans Schönfeld was at work as the expert study director of the Research Department of the World Council of Churches "in process of formation". But it also began among certain far-seeing churchmen in Germany. Eugen Gerstenmeier, who later founded the Evangelical Relief Agency (Evangelisches Hilfswerk) in Germany, writes: "It was from Hans Schönfeld during the war and amid the ruins of Berlin that I first heard news that a large ecumenical aid organization was being planned which would include not only the victims of the aggressor but also the Germans themselves." That must have been even before 20 July 1944 when the attempt on Hitler's life, in which Gerstenmeier was also involved, took place. Bishop Wurm of Württemberg, spokesman for the movement to unite the Evangelical Churches in Germany, published the "Stuttgart Manifesto of Christian Love" on 1 August 1945. This was a call to create a relief agency for the Evangelical Churches in Germany. One year later, the Evangelical Free Churches in Germany joined this effort. At the Evangelical Churches conference in Treysa from 27 to 31 August 1945, when the fundamental decisions were taken for the reordering of the Evangelical Church in Germany, official representatives of the ecumenical movement in Geneva were present and Hans Schönfeld gave a report on the proposed ecumenical relief organization. It was here in Treysa that the Relief Agency of the Evangelical Church in Germany was founded. Bishop Wurm, the newly elected president of the Council of the Evangelical Church in Germany, was appointed as its president and Eugen Gerstenmeier as its director. The latter had escaped death in prison only by some sort of miracle. Yet it was during his imprisonment that, in cooperation with his friend Pölchau, the prison chaplain, he developed plans for an Evangelical relief agency after the war. Scarcely had he been released from prison than he set to work with Bishop Wurm to ensure the realization of this plan. At Treysa in August 1945 the plan was embodied in an organization. The guiding principle was established as follows:

> The first principle is that the urgency of need alone counts. Help is offered irrespective of person, race, religion or political allegiance. Children come first in the Relief Agency's scale of need. Self-help has priority. If we fail to help one another, we have no right to request help from abroad. Whenever our own resources are insufficient, help from abroad must at least be combined with self-help. When people abroad provide us with raw materials which we ourselves lack, we contribute the necessary labour.

One remarkable feature in the creation of the Evangelical Relief Agency is the close interlocking of self-help and ecumenical aid. In retrospect we see that it was quite impossible to separate the two or to consider the one as the cause of the other. In principle, of course, ecumenical aid is always geared to self-help and seeks to stimulate the latter so that the former becomes less and less necessary. On the other hand, this aid from the oikoumene has invariably inspired and triggered off the desire and the energy to help oneself. It is idle to ask what is cause here and what is effect. In ecumenical cooperation self-help and ecumenical aid are inextricably interwoven, quickening and fructifying each other.

In the first three years, i.e. until September 1948, the Evangelical Relief Agency obtained 44,167,260 kilos of gifts from abroad and organized their distribution. These gifts were mainly from churches in all parts of the world but some of them came from non-church relief organizations. In the first year, it was from Switzerland and Sweden especially that immediate neighbourly assistance began to come, until American legislation cleared the way for aid on a massive scale from the USA and then for the many gifts from other European churches. By the processing of raw materials, German labour multiplied the value of these gifts from abroad. As a result of the creation of the German aid agency in all the regional churches, however, large contributions spontaneously started to come in from our own country. Twenty million kilos of foodstuffs and a million articles of clothing were collected in the German Evangelical Churches in the first eight months and the collections on harvest thanksgiving day in October 1945 added a further ten million kilos. We read in an assessment from the year 1948: "The gifts of foodstuffs from Germany were, on the whole, almost equivalent in weight if not in value to the gifts from abroad." In addition to this, in the same period of time German gifts of money amounted to about 180 million German marks. Even when the low value of the German currency at that time is taken into account, this represented a remarkable index of the determination of the Germans to help themselves.

From the beginning, aid was directed to two purposes: to general emergency relief and to church reconstruction. The general emergency aid was divided into programmes to provide basic necessities, food, clothing and medicaments, and programmes to deliver raw materials etc. for processing in German manufacturing and industrial concerns. In this latter area, in particular, aid was especially stimulating and productive so far as self-help was concerned. In his history of the diaconal service and the relief agency, Prof. Beyreuther reports:

> For the years prior to 1948, the following facts should not be ignored. Bare statistics they may be, but indicative nonetheless of the devotion and love lying behind them: it was possible to feed three million children for many weeks, to supply ten thousand youth camps with extra nourishment for their half-million participants, to feed fourteen thousand students, to care for refugees with fifteen hundred full-time helpers, to settle two thousand families, to re-educate and employ twenty thousand homeless victims of the war every year. Support was provided for nearly three thousand homes and institutions of the Inner Mission (Innere Mission). One of the specialist services was the Relief Agency's health service. When the stocks of insulin in the hospitals were practically exhausted and thousands of diabetics were in imminent danger of dying as a result, an urgent appeal from the Relief Agency brought an immediate response in the shape of a large contribution of insulin from the Lutheran World Federation. Churches and church organizations in America sent an unending flow of medicaments, especially things like penicillin which were not available in sufficient quantities in Germany.

In the case of church reconstruction, the first step was to provide the basic necessities for the church life which was now beginning slowly to emerge again. High on the list of priorities were Bibles, hymn books and theological works. Next came the provision of church buildings and assistance in erecting emergency church accommodation in areas where most church buildings had been destroyed. First of all, up to 1948, we received thirty-eight prefabricated church huts which were used as emergency churches. In addition forty-seven temporary "Bartning" churches were erected between Stralsund and Stuttgart; these were prefabricated to a uniform and artistically suitable design, ready for assembly, and erected as the first places of worship in bombed-out areas. Some of them are still standing today and are still used in a spirit of genuine gratitude and religious respect.

I would like now to illustrate the extent to which the Evangelical Relief Agency, as an ecumenical German enterprise of fellowship and solidarity, sparked off fresh initiatives and also, under the challenge of need and distress and inspired by a creative love of the neighbour, had consequences in the services of society in general. The example I shall give is Espelkamp, not far from the Westphalian congregation of Spenge of which I was then pastor.

Espelkamp – an example of ecumenical reconstruction aid

At the request of the World Council of Churches, Birger Forell, chaplain to the Swedish Embassy in Berlin under the Nazi regime and during the war years, paid a visit after the war to the German prisoner of war camps in Britain. In confidential conversations with the camp inmates, the name Espelkamp once cropped up. Hidden in the woods there was a huge German munitions camp with all its corresponding factory facilities: 22 km of solid roads, a rail terminus, 130 solid buildings and halls up to 3,000 square metres large, covering an area of about 250 hectares. Birger Forell had a brainwave. Could this former munitions camp in bombed-out Germany become the site of a new beginning with a truly symbolic significance? He decided to visit Espelkamp. He contacted the British Army of Occupation and the officials of the Evangelical Relief Agency and the Evangelical Church of Westphalia. But it all seemed in vain. British soldiers were already engaged in dynamiting the empty bunkers and halls, dismantling the rail terminus and so on – despite the fact that the German church authorities had already been trying for months to secure the derestriction of the buildings for peaceful uses.

In the end, however, the decisive breakthrough came, almost miraculously. The responsible authorities of the Control Commission provisionally authorized the peaceful use of Espelkamp by the Evangelical Relief Agency. The first work parties of released but homeless prisoners of war from the German East and other refugees moved into the woods around Espelkamp. They were joined by a work team of young American Mennonites doing voluntary service. St Martin of Tours who had shared his cloak with a roadside beggar became the patron saint of the new settlement. In God's name, work was begun on the transformation of a place of war and the manufacture of death into a homestead of peaceful reconstruction. Certain preliminary decisions had to be considered and reached first. Should the now empty halls when restored become centres for a large charitable institution – for children, for the handicapped, for lonely old people? Or should they serve as emergency accommodation for the families of homeless refugees? Or, again, should they be turned into industrial concerns whereby jobs would be created and the economic basis established for the life of those attracted to the place who were now living in the woods and countryside – a bold and far-sighted venture? Although there was opposition to this last plan on various grounds, it was the solution adopted. So it happened that first jobs were created and only secondly the houses for those who found work at Espelkamp. Courageous businessmen came forward and, starting from the smallest beginnings, established firms of the most varied kinds. The result was that people who were eager to find new jobs were attracted to Espelkamp and began at first to live in the woods around in the most primitive conditions imaginable. In this way, out of nothing, indeed out of a place of death, there rose in a few years a rapidly growing settlement, a new town. Today, this town has twenty-four thousand inhabitants, ten thousand jobs, many schools and kindergartens, over a hundred cooperatives, a vigorous cultural life with a theatre and sports centre, as well as – centrally sited – the Thomas Church (Evangelical) and the Liebfrauen Church (Catholic). A large institution of service for the children of latecomer refugees and for old single displaced persons is a reminder of the city's origins and at the same time injects something of the original diaconal spirit and motivation into the life of this modern industrial city.

Is Espelkamp a "Christian" city? Is there such a thing? From the very beginning the idea was, out of a sense of Christian responsibility, to help homeless, jobless, hopeless human beings to find a new basis for existence and then, with open-minded tolerance, give them the freedom to carry out any further development in accord with the principles of the social environment. Espelkamp thus became a city like other cities, a quite "secular city" therefore, but the Christian motivation and purpose remain unforgotten.

Was Espelkamp a legitimate project for Christian development work? Certainly it did not become just an institution for the sick, the disabled, the old and the weak. But does Christian aid and common human responsibility not apply also to human beings who though healthy are still in need? Does it not also apply to the establishment of model institutions of structural social aid? For us, Espelkamp is a far-reaching example in the realm of church and society.

Is Espelkamp an ecumenical project? The name of Birger Forell, the unforgettable initiator, driving force and promoter of the entire project, and the selfless labour of the young Mennonite volunteers from the USA are constantly remembered in Espelkamp as reminders of what has been created in ecumenical cooperation.

Is Espelkamp a church project at all? The church alone could not have carried such a gigantic undertaking to completion. The state, the community, and private entrepreneurs also contributed in decisive ways. At the beginning, however, was the Christian initiative, the venture of Christian faith, and the glow of an ardent love. In the end a contract was established between church and state to create a "development corporation". In the basic contract we read:

> With the object of creating an example showing how an estate formerly devoted to war purposes can be reshaped for peaceful ends based on the spirit of practical Christianity, but also with the object of achieving rational reconstruction work under different conditions by the creation of dwellings in the new community, the Evangelical Church in Germany, the Evangelical Church of Westphalia, and the North Rhine-Westphalia State have on 4 October 1949 founded a corporation. . . . The object of this corporation is to undertake the provision of housing and urban facilities, the establishment of competitive enterprises and the promotion of social and charitable institutions, whereby the former property of the German army, Espelkamp, may become a healthy community, serving the common good, offering refugees and other displaced persons a new home of their own.

Ernst Wilm, who was at that time Präses (Bishop) of the Evangelical Church of Westphalia, jokingly explained to the state representative that this union of church and state was a "shotgun wedding". The child was already born and growing lustily. The parents could no longer ignore the fact. They had to seal the march of events by their marriage.

"Espelkamp is the German problem in a nutshell" – that was how Birger Forell in 1948 described the transformation of the munitions camp into a place of peaceful reconstruction. We see clearly from this microcosm – Espelkamp – in what complex and comprehensive ways Christian love is directed at the individual and society as a whole, at our bodily life as well as our spiritual life, at healthy conditions of work and of life, at both charitable and structural aid – in short, at a comprehensive ministry to needy men and women and at a society which shows respect for our humanity. The secondary school in Espelkamp is called the Söderblom Secondary School. The College of Espelkamp is called the Birger Forell College. People in Espelkamp do not forget what ecumenism achieves.

The founding of Bread for the World

The first contribution from the Evangelical Churches in Germany to the World Council of Churches in Geneva for the ecumenical programme of aid to refugees was made as early as the year 1951. The letter accompanying the donation stated among other things:

> This first donation should also be regarded as an expression of our gratitude for all the help which poured into Germany and came to Evangelical Christians there in recent years from the contributions of churches abroad and their congregations. It is also meant as a token of the steadily growing sense of responsibility which we feel for the need and distress beyond our own frontiers.

At the beginning of 1953, when a natural calamity brought distress and death to hundreds and thousands of people in Holland, Belgium and Britain, the Evangelical Church communities in Germany were swept by a wave of eagerness to help. In 1956, the Evangelical Relief Agency also shared in relief work for Hungary. In a report dating from that year, we read:

> The desperate situation at that time called for exceptional measures. An action team of the Evangelical Relief Agency was sent to Vienna and Budapest. Bishop Dibelius urged action regardless of cost. The German congregations responded with donations to the tune of 3.8 million German marks and subsequent collections and donations produced a further 1.7 million marks. This was an outstanding and encouraging breakthrough for ecumenical aid.

In this gradual way, the transition from a "receiving" to a "giving" church took place. The Protestant campaign Bread for the World was founded in the year 1959, in association with the founding of the great Catholic Lenten offering Misereor, to combat poverty, hunger and sickness in the third world. Two years before that, in 1957, the Synod of the Evangelical Church in Germany had stated officially in its "Declaration on Church and Diakonia in a Changed World":

> Diakonia launches out into the world in all its breadth and depth. To girdle the earth with an ecumenical vision – that is the goal of the

church, not only as the community of faith and prayer but also as the community of hope and love. To be sure, we know of distress in plenty in our own midst. But love cannot stay at home. It breaks through political barriers and climbs over ideological and racial walls. In all countries God has his people and everywhere there are people crying from the depths of need. In Africa and Asia and elsewhere in the world, the churches are calling, together with the peoples among whom they live, for the watchful and unselfish support of the whole Christian family. With the sister churches of the ecumenical movement we would like to vie with one another in the service of love, which reaches out to the ends of the earth. Christians in Germany after the war were at once shamed and blessed by their experience of friendly aid from their Christian sisters and brothers in many countries throughout the world. We are therefore the last to be able to remain silent when cries for help come from all quarters, the last to be able to withhold the response of action. . . The commerce of service never impoverishes us but, on the contrary, opens our windows and doors to fellowship. . . "Cast your bread upon the waters and it will return after many days" (Eccles. 11:1–2).

Bread for the World – in explanation of this choice of title, Christian Berg has written as follows: "*Bread* – this is not only the basic necessity of life but also a word rich in spiritual symbolism; *the world* – this is the object of the love of God and therefore the field in which Christians are to minister and serve; *for* – this means affirmatively, helpfully, constructively, in a way which utterly excludes any hostility." The first great collection took place at Christmas 1959 and was organized jointly by all the Protestant churches and communities in Germany. It had been the custom previously for several separate collections to be made at Christmas. But the challenge to join together in a common ecumenical offering of love, at the Christmas season especially, brought a remarkable response and led to an unprecedented demonstration of voluntary sacrificial giving on behalf of the needy. The first joint collection brought in more than 14 million German marks, of which 780,000 marks came from the Protestant Free Churches; in the following years this total was regularly surpassed and this by a large margin. But far more important than the financial result was the fact that, as a consequence of this collection and the programme developed and extended year by year on the basis of it, there has been in the congregations a growing sense of responsible participation in the ecumenical fellowship of solidarity and love. What was primarily planned as a response of gratitude and love resulted now in a vital and growing identification with suffering throughout the world. People in Germany knew from their own experience what the scourge of hunger meant. Another powerful incentive to this ecumenical diakonia (Christian service) was the determination of the Christian community in Germany to play its part in the establishment of signs of active reconciliation. Not that they thought that all guilt could be purged and a distress which had its roots far back in time be eliminated simply by charitable programmes! But what they *did* know was that when the distant neighbour in the person of the suffering fellow human being knocked at their door and they stretched out a helping hand to offer Christian aid, this could and should be in itself a demonstration of the desire for reconciliation.

The matter did not rest there, however; the public campaign Bread for the World was not the end of the road. In 1960, Dienste in Übersee (Service Overseas), a Commission of the Evangelical Churches in Germany, was founded. The purpose of this Commission was to make professionally qualified experts in every field available to the developing countries for several years' service; to train them and, in accordance with the requests and proposals of the receiving countries, to second them for service. Dienste in Übersee is a type of ecumenical working team located, so to speak, somewhere between mission and diakonia, the purpose of which is to supplement financial and material aid by a total commitment on the part of individual Christians. Up to now, the thousand or so specialists seconded by Dienste in Übersee have been required to serve individually for a minimum of three years. An extra and welcome bonus here is that these "overseas deacons", on their return home, contribute in a most effective way to the promotion of ecumenical awareness and to the process of improving and making more sensitive the mind and conscience of the community.

It was made quite clear by the Synod of the Evangelical Church in Germany in 1968 that the church as a whole was determined to demonstrate its role in the joint programme of ecumenical solidarity by allocating to it resources derived from its income in church taxes. In a declaration on "The Future of the Church and the Future of the World", it was decided:

> The Synod of the Evangelical Church in Germany requests its member churches to set themselves the target of earmarking, in greater measure than hitherto, funds from the budgets of the regional churches and church communities, their agencies and institutions, in order to help eliminate poverty, hunger and distress in the world, and their causes. By a new pattern of priorities, by reviewing operational structures and building plans in the congregations and church districts, but, above all, by stimulating the readiness for sacrifice and self-discipline, to allocate in the first instance 2 percent of all church income for

this purpose, in addition to the income already set aside for these responsibilities and tasks.

Since then, not only the monies donated to Bread for the World but also a considerable part of the domestic resources of the individual regional churches have been available for ecumenical diakonia. In addition to this, there are the further contributions from government resources out of taxation, which are administered by the Protestant Central Agency for Development Aid (Evangelische Zentralstelle), founded in 1962, and made available for church development projects without further state inspection.

The responsibility of coordinating all these church development services falls to the Association of the Churches' Development Services (Arbeitsgemeinschaft kirchlicher Entwicklungsdienst). It is here that decisions are made concerning the appropriate allocation of the monies derived from the various sources (donations, church tax income, government money). The position is summarized in the 1973 Memorandum of the Council of the Evangelical Church in Germany on "The Church's Development Service: a Contribution to Peace and Justice in the World":

> The Church's Development Service began as a spontaneous movement in the Evangelical Church in Germany. The distress and poverty of the peoples in Africa, Asia and Latin America were brought vividly to our notice by the mass media. In this situation, many Christians in Germany recalled their own deep distress in the years immediately following the war and the help they themselves had received at that time. The motivating factors for the first Bread for the World and Misereor campaigns were gratitude and the desire to help our distant neighbours in their sufferings. At the beginning, therefore, emergency relief was very much to the fore. Soon, however, the Development Service was focused on the principle of helping people to help themselves. Projects in the fields of health, education and agriculture are to be so designed that they stimulate and encourage the determination of people to help themselves.

Summary

The decisive change in ecumenical relationships between the Evangelical Church in Germany and the oikoumene began already in the year 1955. At that time Dr W. A. Visser 't Hooft, the WCC general secretary, paid his first visit to the office of the Evangelical Relief Agency. His purpose was to discuss its participation in crucial areas of aid in other countries. The main emphasis of such aid was to be the alleviation of acute distress, the assistance to young churches, and disaster relief. Dr Visser 't Hooft pointed out the range and diversity of tasks and possibilities which existed in many parts of the world for a German Protestantism eager to be of help. It was not just financial gifts and material assistance that were needed, but also people who could help the young churches to take their own destiny in hand. This motivated the German Evangelical Churches to see that the time had come for them to make the transition from "receiving" church to "giving" church. It was in the same spirit that two years later, in 1957, at the Synod of the Evangelical Church in Germany on the theme "Diakonia in a Changed World", the Inner Mission and the Evangelical Relief Agency were united to form a single diaconal agency, Das Diakonische Werk (Ecumenical Diakonia). Basically, the Evangelical Relief Agency had been created only for the limited period of really desperate need, as an auxiliary alongside the Inner Mission. Now the time seemed to have arrived to integrate the two agencies, and for both to merge in the single living stream of diakonia which had flowed in German Protestantism ever since the days of Johann Hinrich Wichern (1808–1881), the founder of the Inner Mission. A special department for ecumenical diakonia was established in Diakonisches Werk in Stuttgart. Here the Bread for the World programme found its organizational anchorage. Here, too, was located the responsibility for the German section of inter-church aid, refugee and world service. In 1960, of its own volition, Diakonisches Werk decided to end all further aid from overseas. At the same time, however, congregations were urged to increase their aid to the German Democratic Republic, the territories east of the Oder-Neisse line, the minority churches in Europe, and churches in the third world. In June 1962, the activities of the Council of Relief Agencies Licensed for Operation in Germany (CRALOG) were solemnly ended. Bishop Dibelius, then president of the Council of the Evangelical Church in Germany, wrote:

> The time has come when support of the kind hitherto given must come to an end. Germany today is certainly still not a rich country. The resources of the churches are limited. With God's help, however, we have reached the point when we can not only look after the daily necessities ourselves but also can and will complete the reconstruction of what was destroyed; can and will tackle, and somehow solve, the enormous problems posed us by the millions of refugees. Over and above this, we have been able to begin once again to turn our eyes towards the churches of other countries and to make our modest contribution to the general aid for the churches, wherever the greatest need prevails. Yet the more we make contact with the needs of these other brothers and sisters, the more it shames us when resources which might be deployed for them are still being used to benefit the Evangelical Churches of Germany. We must now ask our friends, who have

up to now helped us so generously, to reduce this assistance – except for that which can still benefit the eastern part of our homeland. But this turning point in the history of our diakonia ought not to pass by without our having expressed clearly and unambiguously before the whole world our deep gratitude for all that we have received.

Gratitude, thankfulness – that is the beginning of all service. "What have you that you have not received?" asks the apostle Paul (1 Cor. 4:7). That refers both to spiritual gifts and to material gifts, both to what God gives us and to what we owe to him and, for his sake, to our fellow human beings. The story of ecumenical diakonia in post-war Germany is a stirring example of an inter-church aid which, from spiritual beginnings, led on to far-reaching, practical consequences. In this inter-church aid, receiving and giving were and remained intermeshed in a variety of ways. And, in the end, what happened under God's blessing in one place brought forth much fruit also in other places, too.

Does it surprise anyone, then, that having experienced this reality at first hand, I found it impossible to evade the call to work with the Geneva Division for Inter-Church Aid?!

Left: Improved crops, India

Below left: Village development projects in Greece, 1960s

Below: In 1964 for the first time international support was requested for the Mississippi Delta Ministry (USA) designed to serve in an area of grave racial turbulence

Photos: WCC/ J. Taylor, WCC/ P. Williams, Jeremey Hartley/Oxfam

Above: Rural education and development work with Quechua Indians in Bolivia, 1980s

Below right: Supplying water for market gardens, Niger

Inter-Church Aid
and Eastern Europe

Ulrich von Brück

Dr Ulrich von Brück in the following article describes the problems that had to be overcome in securing the full participation of Eastern Europe in the work of inter-church aid, drawing especially (though not exclusively) on the experience of his own country, the German Democratic Republic (GDR). He claims that the Eastern European challenge can be vitalizing.

★ ★ ★

Preliminary personal note

I grew up in a Protestant parsonage in Dresden (now in the German Democratic Republic). In addition to his pastoral ministry, my father was responsible for world mission matters and parish welfare. Two sisters from the Dresden deaconess motherhouse were employed to visit and care for the old and infirm, the lonely and the handicapped. I have never forgotten how on the first day of the month the senior of the two deaconesses, a very imposing personality, would come and greet my father invariably with the same request: "Pastor, I could do with some money." I learned that even in the church nothing can be done without money! Decades later I read from the pen of the director of the Department of Inter-Church Aid, Refugee and World Service (DICARWS) of the World Council of Churches, Dr Leslie Cooke: "Money is a wonderful thing . . . it is simply a commodity by which we ourselves may go in thought and in love and in service where we cannot go personally."

This ecumenical extension of the meaning of money could not yet be clear to me at that time, about 1924, but later, I myself in my ministry as a pastor became involved in worldwide commitments of that kind. I must also mention that in my home parish in the hard post-war inflation years of the twenties, a soup kitchen was set up under my father's supervision and did a lot of good. All that mattered to be given a meal and a seat at table was the individual's need. It was not for instance his membership of the parish that counted. A similar organization had also been set up before, during the severe war winter of 1916. Looking back, one may well say that schemes of that kind had already given rudimentary expression to the idea which is familiar to us now of "sharing resources".

In 1950 I was called by my church, the Evangelical Lutheran Church of Saxony, to take charge of the Inner Mission and Relief Agency. I was reluctant at the time to give up my ministry in a city parish in Dresden. However, I took with me new and, in this form, even unprecedented experiences and wider horizons. All the buildings of my parish and its neighbour (church, parish rooms, parsonage) had been destroyed in the air raid on Dresden on 13 February 1945. For five years I had assembled my congregation for worship and reconstruction in the Roman Catholic Church which had remained intact. I also had many conversations on "ecumenism", "charitable work" and "diakonia" in this period with my brother, the Catholic priest. In the work of my new office the need for food relief throughout the country soon developed. The food supplies came largely from ecumenical sources. The distribution was organized in association with People's Solidarity, an agency run by official social and government personnel. Despite fundamental ideological differences, collaboration on behalf of needy human beings was the main thing. Collaboration of that kind successfully passed its first test at that time. In 1959 the Bread for the World movement was launched on German soil. Until the end of 1980, in addition to my other functions I was involved in this movement as executive secretary for all the Protestant regional and free churches in the GDR. In the course of it, because of the special circumstances within the sphere of the GDR, other quite different and more far-reaching forms of cooperation became necessary and possible. In a rudimentary but successful way we were doing what only came to be discussed for the first time at the DICARWS world consultation in Swanwick, England, in 1966. There the question was raised whether for the sake of ecumenical diakonia and of unlimited service to the world, we should not have to be more open-minded in regard to the other great religious and cultural groups such as Muslims, Hindus, Buddhists, Marxists, secularists. Ought we not to tackle the urgent needs of the world together? At the conclusion of that conference, Dr Leslie Cooke, to whom we have already referred, cautiously summed up the first reflections on this question in this way: "What about all the dangers of syncretism? Of creating a false impression that there is really no difference between us –

nothing distinctive about Christian service? That is involvement with the world – are we ready for that risk?"

At that time DICARWS clearly stood at the beginning of a new conception of its own nature and activities. The Swanwick consultation had as its theme "Inter-Church Aid in the Next Ten Years". Dr Cooke declared: "I think it has become clear to us here that in the next decade we have to move from our conception of service to the world to involvement with, or service in, the world."

Direct participation in the work of DICARWS by the Eastern European area was still very slight at that time. There were various reasons for that. The churches in the area were not at all inactive, however.

What does "Eastern Europe" mean in our context?

Eastern Europe is, to start with, a geographical collective term comprising all the countries from the centre of Europe to the Urals and the Balkan countries with the exception of Greece. Eastern Europe is also, however, understood to mean a domain in which since the end of the Second World War Marxism-Leninism under the leadership of the Soviet Union represents the state ideology and has led to the development of socialist states. Moreover, an element critical of the churches, an atheistic element, cannot be overlooked. The principle of separation between church and state and between church and school is applied. The churches no longer enjoy privileges of any kind.

Eastern Europe can, however, be viewed denominationally or confessionally, and in this respect represents a special region within the ecumenical movement. In the Soviet Union, Bulgaria, Yugoslavia and Romania, the Orthodox Church represents the majority of the Christian portion of the population; in Poland, Czechoslovakia and Hungary, the Roman Catholic Church. Only in the GDR do the churches of Reformation traditions constitute the majority of the Christian part of the population (at present about 40 percent of the total population). Majority here by no means signifies leadership. The other minority churches of the various Reformation traditions in the other countries of Eastern Europe are often more alive, devoted and ecumenically more open-minded than the so-called major churches.

All this must be borne in mind in using the term "Eastern Europe", and it also, of course, shows the difficulty for an individual dealing with the theme. In the course of my ministry over the years I have had the opportunity to visit all the countries of Eastern Europe with the exception of Albania, and have also taken part in DICARWS meetings in Eastern Europe. Quite often on these occasions I was the only German-speaking representative from Eastern Europe, and for a considerable period also the sole representative of the Protestant churches from the GDR. That imposed a special responsibility in every way. Consequently I know many things in Eastern Europe from direct observation. But I do not wish nor can I presume to speak for Eastern Europe as a whole. I want that to be understood and taken into account in reading what follows in this article. Of course for me, experiences and instances from my church ministry in the GDR must be the main thing.

The years since about 1955

The picture today is considerably different from what it was in the first years or at least in the first decade of the work of DICARWS. The friendships and enmities deriving from the war played scarcely any part any more from the ecumenical point of view. Large-scale relief operations, principally by the churches of Switzerland, the Scandinavian countries and the USA, built bridges to the people in countries hardest hit by the war all over Europe. Aid for millions of refugees long claimed special attention. The churches, too, received endless assistance from ecumenical sources for their inner and external reconstruction. The fact that people and churches in the German area were not left out but were ranked among the recipients of such aid on an equal footing, remains unforgettable for all who experienced it, and imposed a lasting obligation on them. The East of Europe figured longer on the receiving side than the West in this respect.

The first post-war period was also marked by undoubted mutual reserve between the West and East of Europe and beyond. This state of affairs has been called the "Cold War", and not without reason, of course. The two centres determining historical developments, Moscow and Washington, of course also influenced the possibilities and limits of church action. Mention must also be made here of the growing difference in economic development. The sphere of influence on the respective national currencies of the American dollar on the one hand and of the Russian rouble on the other made it impossible to act through a common medium of exchange. Travel restrictions between the German Democratic Republic and the Federal Republic of Germany, but also to foreign Western countries, long hampered and prevented direct contact or at least any continuous and direct collaboration in ecumenical agencies. There was collaboration by correspondence from the start, and interest in church life in the East European countries continually increased. Too little was known, however, even in ecumenical circles, about that life, and also about the possibilities available in that area. The lack of representatives of East European churches at meetings of ecumenical agencies gave even visibly an incomplete picture of ecumenism and resulted in incomplete and sometimes one-sided conclusions. This is not the place to go into details and their background, to pass judgment or even to apportion blame. It is only a matter of noting the way things actually were at that time. Special importance also attaches for our purpose to the entry of the Orthodox churches of the East European area, with the exception of Albania, to the World Council of Churches, at the New Delhi Assembly in 1961 and in subsequent years. Mention must also be made in this connection of the diplomatic recognition of the German Democratic Republic attained after many difficulties, and the admission of the two German states into the United Nations. The government of the GDR now saw the possibility of permitting representatives of the churches of their country to participate directly in ecumenical activities on a much larger scale than before. In this way, inter-church activities and types of ecumenical relief work that had developed in the meantime, and were adapted to the economic possibilities of churches in socialist states, could now become known to wider circles of the ecumenical movement. Step by step they were coordinated with and turned to account in the overall work of DICARWS. The obligation to become donors instead of recipients, and to view their own problems in the context of the gigantic problems in the countries of Africa, Asia and Latin America, was also very soon realized in the East European churches and they also desired greater and direct collaboration in the functions of DICARWS within the scope of available possibilities.

As the church of my homeland, the Evangelical Lutheran Church of Saxony, belongs not only to the World Council of Churches but also by its tradition to the Lutheran World Federation, I must mention in this connection that as early as 1952 at the Second Assembly of the Lutheran World Federation (LWF) in Hanover, I had been appointed to the new Commission for Inner Mission established there. It was not possible for us at that time to attend the Assembly itself. From 1955 on, however, starting in Denmark, I was able regularly to take part in the work of that Commission. Later, the function of this Commission was incorporated into the World Service Department of the Lutheran World Federation.

The work of that Commission led to the planning and realization of a first World Conference for Social Responsibility in Springfield, Ohio, USA, which preceded the Third Assembly of the LWF in

1957 in Minneapolis, USA. A second similar world conference in Stockholm, Sweden, in 1963, preceded the Fourth LWF Assembly of the same year in Helsinki, Finland. Thus, though they sprang from a confessional world federation, points of view and functions were developed here which were being given equally serious consideration in the work of DICARWS. The results gained constituted a considerable potential for the World Conference on Church and Society organized by the WCC in 1966 in Geneva.

When in 1962 DICARWS held a world consultation on "What Makes Christian Service Distinctive?" in Nyborg Strand, Denmark, the Bible studies were conducted by the Orthodox Father, Paul Verghese, later Metropolitan Paulos Mar Gregorios. He belongs to the Malankara Orthodox Syrian Church in India, and at that time was working in Geneva in the WCC Division of Ecumenical Action. Among the delegates was a representative of the Ecumenical Council of Churches in Hungary and a representative of the Reformed Church in Yugoslavia, but no representative from any of the Orthodox churches of Eastern Europe and no representative of the churches of the GDR either. The lack of more East European representatives was emphatically regretted by the participants. One of the consultation committees dealt with questions of European concern in the sector of inter-church aid and incipient joint undertakings between European churches. Casa Locarno in Switzerland even then played an important role as an ecumenical meeting and rest centre. It has become for innumerable visitors not only a fine vacation centre in uniquely beautiful scenery, but in it many members of East European churches have gained personal experience of ecumenism and given it shape and form in daily living and eating together. Furthermore, the Casa has prompted the establishment of similar ecumenical vacation centres in several East European churches. In the budget of the DICARWS service programme for 1963 there is, indeed, only a very modest entry, entitled "Ecumenical responsibilities carried by the Division: diaspora and minority churches in Europe". Aid of that kind was at that time chiefly applicable for Western Europe. Three years later, in 1966, when that world consultation was held in Swanwick, England, on the theme "Inter-Church Aid in the Next Ten Years", it was described by Dr Leslie Cooke as the largest and most representative consultation to date, with 239 participants from 78 countries. The representation for the first time of the Roman Catholic Church was especially referred to. The paper presented by the Roman Catholic representative dealt with "The Cooperation of all Christian Churches in the Service of the World Family: Experiment, Sign and Promise Towards the Unity We

Seek". I have already mentioned a striking point from that paper regarding the anticipated and desirable opening out of the work of DICARWS to possible collaboration even beyond the Christian churches of the world. And to quote once again Dr Leslie Cooke on this consultation:

> That we are now caught up to go beyond aid to challenge the structures of church and society, even by the aid we give and the purposes to which we give it, is beyond doubt. . . . The problem of social and economic justice is becoming acute. The interconnection of social, economic and political questions stares us in the face. What does all this mean for our work?

The number of East European delegates at this consultation was three, one each from Poland, Czechoslovakia and Hungary. Once again the GDR was not represented.

The world conference on Church and Society was imminent, and inevitably influenced people's thinking in Swanwick. At this conference in Geneva, almost all East European churches had been represented by delegates, and the presidium included an Orthodox archbishop from the USSR. However, no East European representative was among the heads of sections and working groups. Among the speakers were qualified representatives from the third world, but nobody from Eastern Europe. Let me repeat once again that I mention this not accusingly but because it belongs to the true picture in retrospective analysis and evaluation of the work of DICARWS and of the historical development that had to be gone through. We can now see more clearly than at that time what a many-sided learning process had to be coped with, what barriers, reserves and mistaken assessments had to be overcome. DICARWS was simply sharing in the political and economic development of a divided Europe. For the future, too, it will be a matter of taking into account certain factors of this situation and of incorporating them more successfully into the overall conception of the work of DICARWS. I shall have something further to say on this at the end of this survey.

The world conference on Church and Society was followed within the work of DICARWS by a European consultation in Belgrade in December 1967. I would describe that consultation as the visible breakthrough to pan-European participation, to full Eastern European collaboration in DICARWS. That was expressed by the very fact that the presidium consisted of two East European and two West European representatives and that the role of chairman devolved on a delegate from one of the Czechoslovakian Protestant minority churches. Among the delegates were representatives of all East European countries with the exception of Romania and, for quite different reasons, Albania. Representation of the Orthodox and Protestant traditions was well-balanced. It was the first time a delegate from the GDR had taken part in such a consultation, and I remember clearly the great interest and perceptibly sincere sympathy with which my report on our activity and situation was received in plenary session. Besides myself, a representative of the Roman Catholic Church in the GDR took part, with the status of an adviser. It was observed that personal contacts over-riding all differences and frontiers have just as much value for the work of DICARWS as the elaboration and accomplishment of projects. As a result of the discussions of the section to which I was assigned, a recommendation was submitted to the plenary which to a considerable extent was based on experiences which had already been gained and used in practice for many years in East European churches and relief organizations; this was to the effect that wherever necessary and possible, relief agencies and churches should cooperate with corresponding state and interstate agencies as loyal and critical partners.

Experience has confirmed that regular and extensive active collaboration of East European churches in line with the purposes of DICARWS was and continues to be possible only in appropriate cooperation with corresponding state or social agencies. The work of the Bread for the World movement supported by all Protestant regional and free churches in the GDR, was able to involve such collaboration from the start, and has consolidated it loyally. That happened first of all with the Red Cross, but also with the GDR Afro-Asian Solidarity Committee and in particular here with its Vietnam Committee. In addition, in individual cases there were GDR agencies of external and inter-German trade. In the course of time increased opportunities arose for direct cooperation with ecumenical service agencies in the receiving countries and the central offices in Geneva. Since, as has already been mentioned, the currency situation did not and does not allow the transfer of cash to Geneva, collaboration has consisted and continues to operate chiefly in the domain of material aid, and here again primarily in the medical and health sector and in the domain of disaster relief in earthquakes, famine, drought and their consequences. Only new manufactured products from the GDR form the content of the relief supplies sent. Regard for the planned economy involves certain directives here, and also limits which have to be respected. The Red Cross or the Solidarity Committee served as intermediaries for the GDR Bread for the World movement and I was more than 'once able personally to accompany these relief supplies and to deliver them to agencies in the receiving country for further appropriate dispatch. In this way the source of these donations could be made clear and shown to be financed from church resources. Receptions and talks up to prime ministerial level did in fact result from this. Even during the consultation in Belgrade I was able to use the opportunity for talks with representatives of the Yugoslav Red Cross – all the more urgently as, a few days earlier, an earthquake had seriously affected the region around Debar in the south of the country. The even more devastating earthquake in Skopje, Yugoslavia, in 1963 had also prompted the immediate despatch of considerable aid and materials for the rebuilding of a children's clinic, financed from church funds in the GDR. And similar experiences such as prompted the activities of the Bread for the World movement in the GDR also inspired action by other East European member churches in particular cases, for example in the USSR or in Hungary. In this way, ecumenical sharing of resources has recently become a thoroughly discussed and topical theme within the East European region. The number of endeavours to practise that kind of sharing both within Eastern Europe and also throughout the ecumenical movement, as far as existing circumstances allow, is continually increasing.

The Belgrade consultation took place in the run-up to the WCC Fourth Assembly in Uppsala, Sweden, in 1968. One of the particularly striking events in Uppsala was a general session of the Assembly one evening in the great hall of the university. The chair was taken by Dr Martin Niemöller, one of the then presidents of the World Council of Churches. The hall of the university was filled to capacity. In one of the volumes of reports we read of this evening session:

> One of the speakers is a delegate from the GDR. "The Church of Jesus Christ is to bring the message of God's love to the world; this love cannot stop at platonic declarations but must become action," insisted Oberlandeskirchenrat Ulrich von Brück from Dresden, in an address which like further contributions of the evening from Pastor Kotto from Cameroon and Miss Janet Lacey from London, referred to the work and aims of DICARWS. . . . Particular interest was shown by church representatives from all over the world in the reports by von Brück, director of the Bread for the World movement in the GDR, on its relief work to date. He reported, for example, that the Protestant churches in the GDR in cooperation with the Red Cross in the GDR have worked out forms of collaboration in ecumenical Christian service which have already made assistance possible in about 125 cases to a total value of about 13 million marks and a two million marks contribution through the GDR Afro-Asian Solidarity Committee for Vietnam.

In the meantime, the total amount of all collections so far for Bread for the World in the churches of the GDR has reached 80 million marks.

An instance of that kind was, of course, only intended to make clear how soon – though in different circumstances to those in the headquarters in Geneva – the task of DICARWS was seen as inspiring and imperative in East European churches. These churches, too, wished to become giving rather than receiving churches. The refugee problem, hunger, the need for economic and social justice, had emerged ever more clearly as *the* problem of the countries of Africa, Asia and Latin America. Very soon, therefore, people began to say that the worldwide problems of East-West relations were not the only ones, but that those of North-South relations needed just as much to be clearly perceived. The overcoming of the antithesis between rich and poor comes ever more unmistakably into focus as decisive for the future of the world. To identify the causes of economic and social injustices, to overcome them and establish healthy and just structures, must with increasing urgency become the subject of DICARWS consultations side by side with individual relief cases and projects for active intervention which are still as necessary as ever. To advance further here all WCC member churches are needed, whichever region they belong to and whatever the social structure in which they carry out their Christian service. There will, of course, continue to be differences of insights and differences of emphasis in matters of detail.

The possibilities of action and of cooperation will also continue to be diverse. Nevertheless, there can be no doubt any more regarding joint thinking and involvement of all WCC member churches even in a field of work like that of DICARWS. Already by 1962 in this connection at one of the DICARWS consultations the noteworthy statement was made that "inter-church aid must truly be mutual". And another remark that was also made very early on points in the same direction: "Christian service does not ask: 'are you a faithful Christian?' and it is free from all political ties, except the tie with Christ." Certainly necessary forms of cooperation also mean increased consideration of others; they also, however, require increased trust, which must be unqualified unless there is proof to the contrary. That applies to internal ecumenical work but even more to cooperation with non-ecclesiastical, non-ecumenical partners.

I am convinced that the number of favourable examples of such cooperation has been constantly increasing. And the more the World Council ensures that its departments think and work globally in responsibility for humankind as a whole the greater the justification for regionalization within its overall conception. Very early on in DICARWS, the idea was expressed that more responsibility for the work of the department should not mean more centralization. In regard to the application of the project system, it had been questioned whether it should be a matter of the projects being carried out *by* the department, or whether it should not more correctly be a case of the projects being carried out by the churches *through* the department. At the same time the projects, though differing in the manner of realization, could all be entered and figure in the CICARWS statement of accounts as activities falling within its total scope, as was also finally possible, we are glad to say, in the case of the activities carried out through Bread for the World in the GDR. Regular assessment of the project system will have to remain a recurring item on the agenda of CICARWS. And as regards Eastern Europe it will always be important how Inter-Church Aid can maintain and continually reshape links inside a divided Europe. Inventiveness and imagination are constantly in demand here. Consequently I am very pleased that my contribution is followed by an article by the New Zealander, Dr Alan Brash, of whom I thought highly as director of CICARWS, dealing with the process of regionalization, and that Jean Fischer, who was also CICARWS director, also has something to say on this important topic.

Subsequent CICARWS meetings were held in Yugoslavia and Bulgaria in 1973, in Warsaw in 1974 with special reference to contacts with the Conference of European Churches, and again in Sofia, Bulgaria, in 1982. In each case the purpose was renewed encounter with the churches of Eastern Europe and information about the possibilities of practical ecumenical diakonia that had been developed in the meantime. To make full use of the possibilities existing in that region and to incorporate them more and more into the overall planning and function of CICARWS was in each case an important topic for discussion.

Within the period assigned for this survey, it was a first substantial advance when the activities developed by the East European churches were mentioned in the CICARWS reports and were increasingly recognized as integral parts of the idea and work of CICARWS. A second step forward came when, in the case of suitable projects, the attempt was made to ensure participation of East European churches in carrying out the project, usually by their sharing in the delivery and payment of material requirements. This quite often meant a certain complication of the whole transaction and delay in performance and completion of the particular project. The materials required could not always be obtained immediately because of the planned economy; the transport channels of non-ecclesiastical agencies had to be taken into account, which necessitated additional coordinating discussions on the part both of senders and recipients. Church and ecumenical service agencies in the particular receiving country had accordingly a special part to play. Nevertheless, such attempts were necessary for the sake of setting up a comprehensive operation, and led to very favourable results. Even as well-oiled a "machine" as CICARWS naturally needs, has constantly to be open to exciting, stimulating and continual inventiveness and imagination. I have always regarded the special situation of Eastern Europe as a salutary disturbing factor, at least in the sense that it is not just a case of the machine simply functioning. And it did in fact become increasingly clear that what was at stake was not merely material aid provided by East European member churches. I refer here to the lively exchange of spiritual experience between the East European churches, exchange of literature for the benefit in particular of training centres for various forms of Christian service, holiday offers in the East European region – open also to guests from West European or overseas churches – and the exchange of theological and practical experience relating to various features of the churches' diakonia in a developing socialist society. All these are partial aspects within the one Christian service incumbent on all of us. Here we can constantly learn from each other to our mutual enrichment through difference of gifts and potentialities.

Concluding remarks

Some attempt must finally be made to sum up what I have presented from my own personal experience and from collaboration in CICARWS over a number of years. What will be the significance of the Eastern Europe region for CICARWS in the future? Eastern Europe has its special features as every other region has. It contains elements favourable to Christian service, but also others that impose limits to it. The latter may in many respects be more conspicuous than in other regions. The learning process for the churches in Eastern Europe of identifying, affirming and performing their function in a socialist social order, is not yet at an end. Moreover, the state agencies are also involved in a learning process of that kind. In 1983, the 500th anniversary year of Martin Luther's birth, for example, the churches and GDR state mutually acknowledged that in a quite new way they had come to realize and put into practice the meaning and value of the motto "Daring to trust" – this was the key theme of the various "Kirchentags" celebrating the occasion. Here, too, new possibilities and consequences for the future are apparent which ought also to be taken note of outside the East European region.

I think that various kinds of experience have taught that collaboration with non-church agencies in the interest of the people one is trying to serve ought not to remain an exceptional case. I have always thought that it is really providential that in Geneva the offices of the World Council of Churches and of some Christian world confessions are situated not very far from those of the International Committee of the Red Cross and the League of Red Cross and Red Crescent Societies. I also know, of course, that all kinds of contacts do in fact exist and are cultivated between these offices. Nor is there any question but that the fundamental approach of all ecumenical, that is to say church, activities therein has to be the gospel of Jesus Christ which consequently determines the nature of possible and appropriate cooperation.

But, however thankful we may be that the staff of CICARWS do excellent work in Geneva with great dedication and daily application, it must nevertheless also continue to be clear that it is an instrument of the WCC member churches and the ecumenical movement. The composition of the staff, of the Commission and of the various sub-sections must reflect the worldwide fellowship of the WCC. Tried and tested working structures have constantly to be reviewed and adapted to new situations. All this is to be perceived as an ever new enrichment. East European churches have for their part quite often been able to act as stimulus and example, just as CICARWS for its part has helped the East European churches to find their own identity and elicit their own activity. What we envisage today under the heading of "sharing and healing" as an essential concept of ecumenical understanding and action for the whole world aptly applies to the work of CICARWS. It is a matter here of what Ernst Lange, a very committed member of the WCC staff, who died young, once expressed in this way: "I should wish to have the courage to build bridges even where bridge-building is unpopular, right across all fear, all self-righteousness. I ask you, Lord, for courage to build bridges." That the "Eastern Europe" phenomenon again and again appears even for the WCC and its agencies to be a disquieting element, was brought home to me during the very days when I was writing this article as I read in one of the November 1984 issues of the *Ecumenical Press Service* how yet again – this time from the British side – "the East Europe policy of the WCC" was being attacked and defended. This is not the place to inquire in detail into the rights and wrongs of such criticism. But the mere fact of an article of that kind is noteworthy in itself.

CICARWS is integrated into the Programme Unit on Justice and Service. In view of contemporary worldwide thinking and needs, favourable and unfavourable aspects linked with the keyword "Eastern Europe" cannot fail to be attentively followed, taken seriously and as far as possible incorporated into the overall concept of ecumenical responsibility, ecumenical thought and action. CICARWS was and remains to that extent, therefore, a particularly important testing ground.

Regional Responsibility: its Joy and Pain

Alan A. Brash

In this chapter, before those which give some survey of developments in different regions, Dr Alan Brash gives a far from uncritical account of the processes which led to the devolving of the power of decision-making increasingly to the regions. He sees the process as far from complete. The objectivity of his judgment may be held to derive from his unique experience as a former national council general secretary, regional conference staff member, director of Christian Aid (Britain), of CICARWS and finally WCC deputy general secretary.

★ ★ ★

I am grateful that Kyaw Than and Samuel Amissah, people more appropriate than me, tell later in this volume something of the birth and early struggles of the East Asia Christian Conference and the All Africa Conference of Churches. They are the right people for it, and they set me free to tell a more personal story, as one deeply involved in both sides of the new relationship brought by the regionalization of the ecumenical service enterprise, – and as one often involved in the inevitable tensions that resulted. I can only tell my story as I felt and lived it, and nobody but I will be responsible for the opinions expressed.

As is emphasized at the beginning of this book, the WCC, growing out of the earlier ecumenical enterprises and being conceived through the Second World War and born in 1948, was inevitably centred primarily in Europe and North America. In those early years, the Council constituency being what it was and with the agony of Europe still running red, the service task to hand was with millions of displaced people, thousands of devastated cities, the replacement of hundreds of churches and all the rest that followed war's horrors. Yes, it was inevitable.

But the gospel being what it was, that situation could not be tolerated for long by a body claiming to be called to serve "the whole of the inhabited earth". For there was poverty, and starvation and devastation beyond measure in the rest of the world. Urgent voices within the WCC began to press for a worldwide response. One thinks of Leslie Cooke, Robert Mackie and many more. And others, outside WCC structures but within its fellowship, were heard with increasing uneasiness – missionary leaders like John Coventry Smith, Virgin Sly, Eugene Smith and Alford Carlton and especially Asians and Africans like D. T. Niles, M. M. Thomas, Samuel Amissah and Z. K. Matthews. Even earlier, Bishop Azariah and Sarah Chakko had spoken words to disturb any exclusive concentration on Europe.

But there were plenty of obstacles. Where would the resources come from? How should it be organized? How would a truly ecumenical service enterprise relate to the vast missionary programme which was itself heavily committed to service projects?

So the change came only slowly. An early and significant step in 1950 was the joint appointment by the International Missionary Council (IMC) and the WCC – still separate bodies – of the Rev. Rajah Manikam of India, as a kind of roving ecumenical secretary for Asia. Rajah Manikam did an apparently modest, but eventually explosive, job. He simply moved from one Asian country to another and introduced the churches to one another! Previously most Asian churches had known their Western missionary supporters far better than they had known the churches of the neighbouring countries. Their privileged leaders may have met one another briefly at world conferences, but their close bread-and-butter relations were with Western churches.

But Rajah Manikam, perhaps more than anyone else, began to break down the walls. I well remember his visit to Christchurch, New Zealand. His addresses held us spellbound, and when you analyzed them they were essentially a catalogue of facts and figures, and personal experiences about churches in one Asian country after another. This was news par excellence in our country, where we still spoke of the Mar Thoma Church in India as a "younger church" and regarded Indonesian churches as needing our assistance! I am sure it was the same throughout the region. How were these churches to be brought closer together? How could they feel really involved in one another's life?

While the ecclesiastical powers at world level were pondering Manikam's reports, the overseas mission people in the United Presbyterian Church in the USA became impatient for action. John Coventry Smith records the story in his book *From Colonialism to World Community*.[1] In his experience an idea had been launched in

---

[1] Philadelphia, Geneva Press, 1982.

1953 by an Asian Christian asking how his church could be involved in ecumenical mission. John consulted William Decker, assistant general secretary of the IMC, who told him that the IMC could not start such a programme, but that if some of its member bodies did so, and asked for IMC help, it could be given.

So, encouraged by Charles Lebber, his general secretary, John called together a meeting in Hong Kong to discuss that original question. Most of the churches that participated were united churches, related to the US Presbyterians, but the Congregationalists and Methodists also sent observers. Dr Coventry Smith comments that all of the Asians present knew him but they did not know each other. They began to think of ways to help each other in mission, and the first inter-Asian missionary exchange was finalized on the spot.

A second meeting was held in Hong Kong in 1955. Nobody came specially from the USA, but some American missionaries were involved. It was there that they launched the Asia Council on Ecumenical Mission and decided to invite other Asian churches to join. Bishop Enrique Sobrepena of the United Church of Christ in the Philippines was elected chairman. The leaders of the world bodies reacted negatively, and Charles Ranson of the IMC even sent a letter to Asian national Christian councils warning them against the new body. Max Warren, a prominent member of the IMC, attacked the idea of Asian countries exchanging missionaries.

So was called the very important meeting in Bangkok in 1956 where the issues were first fought over, and then clarified. I was present at that meeting. My main memories of it are two. It was the first time I had ever spoken in such company. I spoke in support of the new initiative, and I will always remember the face of my beloved mentor Visser 't Hooft as he watched me differing from him. I think he was more amused than angry. But my second memory is of the statesman-like way that same leader eventually changed his mind and said so. "As in so many ecumenical conferences, the sinners' bench has moved to the other side of the room, and Charles Ranson and I are sitting on it."

Before the meeting dissolved, it had been unanimously agreed that the following year there would be a conference to which all Asian churches related to the WCC would be invited. This historic assembly was held at Prapat, Sumatra, Indonesia in 1957. "Everybody" was present, with the sad exception of Rajah Manikam who perhaps reasonably felt that the location between two warring armies was inappropriate! However, the armies, being Indonesian, left us alone.

The leadership at Prapat clearly took shape in the persons of Bishop Enrique Sobrepena of the Philippines and D. T. Niles of Ceylon – with Kyaw Than and M. M. Thomas not far behind. I personally shared a bedroom with D. T. Niles and John Coventry Smith – and in ways somewhat beyond my understanding, I emerged from that meeting as one of the three staff members of the proposed body – the East Asia Christian Conference (EACC).

Materially, and programme-wise, that was made possible because Leslie Cooke, also present, offered EACC from WCC Inter-Church Aid funds ten thousand dollars a year to support a secretary. The Asians to my delight insisted on it being a secretary for mission *and* service. They also insisted, to our complete surprise, that the Asian region was to include Australia and New Zealand. For me personally the result was that in the next seven years until 1964, I not only travelled the length and breadth of Asia on ecumenical programmes of service and mission and tried to continue my regular work for the New Zealand National Council of Churches, but I went up and down my own country proclaiming not so much the needs of Asia, but the urgent need of New Zealand to become aware of its neighbourhood. It moved me deeply: not that I was awarded a Queen's decoration, but that I was awarded it for "having changed New Zealand's image of Asia".[2]

For me they were eleven incredible years in which I served EACC – for the first seven based on my New Zealand job, and thereafter full-time in Singapore. It was a period of a decentralized secretariat, but with great authority in the hands of our beloved, if non-letter-writing, secretary, D. T. Niles.

But some mighty problems remained for WCC Inter-Church Aid, and especially for Leslie Cooke. Should he support a staff member of EACC, and also an Asia secretary in Geneva? Should it be the same person? Above all, how could he handle the suddenly great financial resources of "cricket teams" of service agencies to Asian churches without totally annoying the major mission boards which were deeply involved in service but with over-stretched resources?

An uneasy compromise was reached. A consultation at Herrenalb, Germany, created some restrictions on the ecumenical service outreach to areas outside Europe. The criteria established were inevitably labelled "The Herrenalb Categories". They were organizationally understandable, but were eventually recognized as a bureaucratic hindrance to the service potential within the

---

[2] Dr Brash was made OBE.

ecumenical movement. It is not useful to recount their full text here – sufficient to say that they represented an endeavour to confine WCC service involvement to disasters, to refugees, to churches without missionary support, and generally to keep the service agencies out of the areas of the major missionary societies.

Of course, though an EACC secretary for mission and service had been appointed in 1957, and the Herrenalb Categories accepted in 1955, the basic issues of regionalization had not really been faced, let alone solved. All projects from the third world which had to be screened by the local national Christian council were nevertheless finally accepted or rejected by Geneva. Area secretaries for each continent were clearly necessary there to do the work and make the final proposals. And without making negative implications about their competence, commitment or sensitivities, in fact those secretaries were for many years mostly from the West.

The result was a long period in which the WCC handled a growing volume of emergency, refugee and project requests with considerable sensitivity. But the almost inevitable slowness of the response by the church agencies after the sometimes tedious "Geneva process" led the asking churches to take their really urgent and priority needs not to the WCC at all, but either to their missionary partner or directly to one of the more affluent service agencies. These latter, despite their protestations of loyalty to the ecumenical process, were often only too eager to exercise their independent power by direct dealing. At that time, it was estimated by those closely associated with the work that 90 percent of the flow of compassionate funds from Western churches bypassed the WCC structure.

The WCC Inter-Church Aid Division made valiant efforts to improve the project list system and respond more effectively and more promptly to disaster appeals. The revision of the system was on nearly every agenda. Increasingly the area secretaries personally came from the regions for which they were responsible.

In the "Geneva process" people in the regions were increasingly involved. For Asia this included both the Asia secretary of WCC Inter-Church Aid and the EACC secretary for mission and service. The team relationship established is evidenced by the fact that in a gap of three months at the WCC Asia desk, I was brought in to maintain the work there.

An illustration of the difficulties in administration and responsibilities is naturally seen in the programmes in Vietnam. The major ecumenical service programme in that war-torn country was very much based in Asia itself. The Asian Christian Service, as it was called, was made up of volunteers (up to forty in number at certain stages) all of whom were recruited in the region. And the main link with churches worldwide was with the EACC secretary now based in Singapore (who visited the programme at least once every two months over several years) and with a Vietnamese secretary, Nguyen Tang Canh, based in Geneva.

Parenthetically let it be said that Canh was a Buddhist, and the WCC received a lot of flak from people around the world who resented our using a man of another faith in a Christian-based programme. But the WCC never made a more appropriate appointment. The image of Christians in many Vietnamese circles, after the French and American presence, was far from good. And we needed someone who both had good contacts in Vietnam and with Vietnamese in Paris, and spoke the language. His care for the suffering ones was emphatically not inferior to that of any Christian.

But of course, though funds were raised from the Asian churches (sometimes at substantial sacrifice) the world ecumenical resources were needed, and therefore the Division had to be, and was, totally involved. The American churches naturally felt they had to be separately and visibly present, so they created their own programme, Vietnam Christian Service.

Some of the pressures involved are illustrated also by another incident. One of the major Western agencies, with vast financial resources as well as incredibly strict administrative procedures and programme limitations, approached the EACC with an offer of help. They indicated that they would gladly locate a representative of their agency in Asia, and that that person, being fully trained in their procedures, would guide the Asian churches in drawing up programme requests in such a way that the agency would be able to accept and fund them. However well-intentioned this offer may have been, the EACC saw it as putting a Western straitjacket on the Asian churches, and allowing their development and programmes to be shaped by Western administrative structures, and, in fact, put under Western control. Under the leadership of D. T. Niles, the EACC firmly rejected the offer.

Gradually the power of decision-making *was* shifted into the regions, certainly as far as the main project selection was concerned. By their very nature (of urgency and size) disaster situations are handled still by the necessarily centralized processes of Geneva, with its agency contacts. Clearly regional people are involved in programme decisions, but administratively funding decisions are centrally handled.

It would be tedious as well as difficult for me to recount the detailed steps in the process. Suffice it to say that for project endorsement all decisions are made by ecumenical groups in the regions. A particular church that wants support in Asia, for example, has to get clearance from its own national Christian council, and then the WCC seeks clearance from a regional screening group (which WCC area staff attend and, by invitation, a service agency representative may also attend) and that is a final decision. Of course it remains that even when Geneva lists the project, the decision of an agency or church which has resources to provide finance is clearly in its own power. Thus for the church in Asia, the dilemma remains; should it seek help through the ecumenical process, or should it use its influence and go direct to its missionary supporting agency – or even to a service agency – to get a privileged and quicker response? Let it also be clear – the same temptation remains with the mission board or service agency to decide against or for working ecumenically or having greater power in its own hands by responding to direct appeals. Sometimes one feels that the ecumenical bond and commitment are strong, but often they do not stand the strain in day to day operations. The way we seek money, and the way we spend it, often speak louder than our speeches on ecumenical occasions.

Meanwhile there has been a new attempt to grapple with the ecumenical relationships between churches, in the widest understanding of what it means to share resources. This has meant several things. On the part of the WCC structure, it has meant a more comprehensive drawing together of a number of programme sub-units previously tending to be in competition with one another for the material resources of the member churches, and obliging them to subsume their needs under a more comprehensive concept of sharing. In a less structural sense, it involves looking at the reality and possibility of ecumenical sharing not only in financial terms. This means accepting a clear recognition that the materially affluent churches with money to share need the personal and spiritual gifts of churches that do not. It struggles to find the implications of recognizing every church as being both a donor and a receiver. Until a church knows itself as in need of receiving, its giving must be less than Christian. However difficult that concept is to implement, the WCC has to struggle with it.

So the process of regionalization goes through a whole series of stages:
- first, the centralization of power of decision;
- second, the sharing of that power;
- third, the regionalization of the power of selection, but the agency power of decisions about money;
- finally, the struggle for a situation in which every church is aware, and is treated accordingly, as a church with resources to

share, and every church is seen as in need of major help from others.

As far as the WCC and the regional ecumenical agencies are concerned, the third stage has been reached. The final stage is understood and elaborated, even if not yet much lived by. But clearly it is an implication of the gospel and we cannot escape that. We will frequently violate the koinonia that it espouses, but the call for a greater obedience will not go away.

Asia

Kyaw Than

In his candid review of the significant developments of inter-church aid in the Asian scene Prof. Kyaw Than of Burma combines searching descriptions of the challenges that a new order in much of Asia brought to traditional Christian work, with heartening accounts of the practical result of the growth of ecumenical commitment both regionally and globally.

★ ★ ★

I had the privilege of being introduced to some of the key personalities who led the thinking of the World Council of Churches in the early years following its inauguration, when I reached Geneva in 1950 as a greenhorn who had been invited to serve as Asia secretary of the World's Student Christian Federation (WSCF, later to become the World Student Christian Federation).

Dr Robert Mackie, the then director of Inter-Church Aid of the World Council of Churches, was also the chairman of the WSCF. At times I was invited to take part in meetings dealing with inter-church aid matters. On such occasions I often heard Robert Mackie emphasizing repeatedly the point that inter-church aid was a *permanent* obligation of the church. He was already giving a lead in making WCC policy-makers realize that ecumenical action in service was theologically a continuing obligation of the churches, and that its programme must well go beyond the cooperative actions for reconstruction of the churches in Europe.

WSCF's background of key WCC leaders such as Dr Visser 't Hooft and Dr Robert Mackie surely deepened this sensitivity towards the need as well as the perspectives of the churches, and even larger human communities, beyond Europe. Among churches outside Europe and North America, the churches in Asia had raised their voices through articulate spokesmen, questioning patterns of Christian service adopted by churches of the West as they reach out to regions beyond their own familiar environment.

Human misery and need encountered by Christian missionaries in Asia and elsewhere had prompted the sending churches' response in deeds of loving service. Schools for education along adapted patterns of the West, orphanages to take care of the needy and hospitals to minister to the sick were looked upon as natural corollaries of mission. (But there had also been veterans like Adoniram Judson, the famous missionary to Burma, who looked upon schools, for example, as distractions of missionary labour from the essential priority task of direct proclamation of the gospel.)

Encounter with the challenges to the Christian's loving witness in strange social and cultural settings provided the church with concrete theological issues in the ecumenical movement.

At the Second Assembly of the World Council of Churches, held in Evanston, USA, in 1954, D. T. Niles of Ceylon in his famous meditation on "Summons at Midnight" shared his very significant insights. He said:

> Too exclusively and too easily we conceive the Christian task as that of seeking and finding the lost, so that we are constantly preoccupied about going out to do it. We do not sufficiently realize that the evangelistic situation is again and again that of being surrounded and sought after and questioned. There are those who are knocking at the door of the church; and they are not merely the hungry, the homeless, the refugee, the displaced person, the outcast; there are at the church's door also every type of community – nations, races, classes, political groupings – knocking for different reasons. Some are asking for "food", others simply ask what kind of people live in this house in which a light shines at midnight, and still others come just to shake their fist in the faces of those who keep a light burning but have no "food".
>
> For it is true that so often there is no "food" in the house. The church is expecting no callers and has laid in no supplies. With what "food" it had, it has just managed to feed its own children. It has sufficient obedience not to put out the light in the window, but it does not have sufficient expectancy to believe that anybody will come.

Preoccupation with service institutions that developed in the missionary enterprise led Asian churchmen to raise serious questions about their validity, theologically speaking. Either those service institutions had become very alien in support arrangements, in personnel and orientation, or these had become settings for dissociation from the spiritual and worship life of the church. P. O. Philip of India in his article in *The International Review of Missions* contended that in Christian ashrams (the humble indigenous centres) ". . . a truly Indian way of service has been found".[1] In another article along similar lines, in the same quarterly

---

[1] *The International Review of Missions*, Vol. XVIII, No. 70, April 1929.

in 1938, T.-C. Chao of China shared his perspective. He stated that the Christian movement in China had been dominated by the Christian service institutions.

> They reached out far and wide, but the Christian movement was weak at the centre. The Christian intelligentsia serving in these insti-tutions were lost to the Church as they ceased to associate themselves in worship and spiritual fellowship with the Church.[2]

Reverting back to Adoniram Judson and Burma, it was an irony that in spite of Judson's antipathy to schools in his preoccupation with Christian mission, quite a few educational institutions (including one of higher education, later incorporated by the state-supported university) were named by those who came after him, in his memory!

Coincidentally, the years immediately following the adoption of inter-church aid as part of the WCC programme were marked by developments in Asian history which raised basic questions about the form of service the churches had developed over the years in the continent as in Burma. Asian nations were regaining their independence. Provision for education alongside national values and goals through increased number of schools, caring for the sick through hospitals, and looking after social service needs of needy persons in their different conditions, were asserted as state responsi-bilities. Private bodies (especially those with foreign connection and sectarian motivation) need not be substitutes of the state to provide these services. With such views the newly independent states with socialist sensitivities took over the service institutions of the churches.

The East Asia Christian Conference (EACC) which was estab-lished as an organ of continuing cooperation among the churches and Christian councils in East Asia, including Australia and New Zealand, studied the need for new forms of service in the historical situation of the region.

What was needed in this changing situation in the field of Chris-tian service was not just some special ministry or some form of experiment but a radical reappraisal of the forms of service of the churches. A series of consultations on "new forms of service and participation" was developed by the EACC. This should not be seen as an exclusive Asian ecumenical endeavour. After all EACC developed out of the joint East Asian secretariat of the World Council of Churches and the International Missionary Council. There was continuing dialogue between EACC and these world

---

[2] *The International Review of Missions*, Vol. XXVII, No. 108, October 1938.

bodies on issues of Christian service, fellowship, and proclamation of the message. The so-called sending churches in the West and the young churches of Asia were getting new opportunities for dialogue on inter-church aid within the fellowship of the WCC. Such frank and creative sharing was also facilitated by relationships of trust and affection between EACC executives and inter-church aid personalities of the WCC such as Robert Mackie, Leslie Cooke and Edgar Chandler, of the formative years. Later D. T. Niles became a president of the World Council of Churches while the EACC mission and service secretary, Alan Brash, went to Geneva to head up the WCC Division of Inter-Church Aid, Refugee and World Service, and become subsequently a deputy general secretary of the whole Council itself. In the current period Samuel Isaac, another inter-church aid secretary of the Christian Conference of Asia (successor to EACC), moved to the WCC to also serve in CICARWS.

The naming of persons and references to the traffic between the regional and world bodies are testimonies to the creative exchange of ideas and persons within the ecumenical movement. Such relationships also facilitated frank exchanges even when convictions and perspectives might not always coincide.

Referring back to one large issue regarding the consideration of new forms of service by the Asian churches, it may not be inaccurate to say that such cross-fertilization between the regional and the world ecumenical bodies contributed towards the exploding of traditional concepts of the churches' service.

The changing historical situation in Asia was providential in this development. The churches primarily of the West, though in partnership with the related Asian churches, were devoting substantial resources to the maintenance and extension of the service institutions. The administration and maintenance of these took a substantial portion of the energy and human as well as material resources of both the sending and the receiving churches. The minority community of Christians surrounded by people of other faiths in the same nation were seen by the latter as having influence and opportunity out of proportion to their numbers and capacity within the country. These medical, educational and social service institutions became, in a number of places, bones of contention or objects of suspicion and even envy for those sensitive about developing integrated national policy and programme.

The churches through these facilities were sometimes seen as competing with state programmes or sowing seeds of dissension among the sectors of the population being served.

On the part of some Christians in both the sending and receiving countries, a sense of possessiveness and monopoly crept in. Such Christians in the country began to feel that they deserved priority attention in gaining benefit of the service rendered. Instead of being servants for the needs of society at large, they began to behave as patrons to whom other people and even the state owed debts of gratitude.

The institutions often being introduced and basically supported from churches abroad could take on forms which were beyond indigenous scales of resources and character. Instead of bilateral and unequal exchanges of thought and experience, the ecumenical setting called the partners in service to consider the traditional concepts and practices in a more comprehensive and objective atmosphere.

Forms of service congruent with convictions, character, and scale of resources of the Christian community in the country where the service was being rendered, were seen as the need of the times in spite of the magnitude of response that could be proposed through disproportionate assistance secured from outside sources. This was not to be unconcerned about the extent of service that might be needed. It had more to do with the authenticity of service and the manner of devising a way to meet that need, as well as with the long-range effect it might have on the role of the church in society at large in Asia.

There were, of course, instances of indigenous service efforts manifesting in the form of key large institutions. Union Christian College at Alwaye in India was the result, humanly speaking, of corporate ecumenical undertaking by indigenous lay people who were under a common spiritual discipline. In another context, there was the All Japan Peasant Union which Dr Kagawa helped to, found. His efforts to meet the needs of workers towards the close of the nineteenth century in Japan resulted in the founding of the Association for Formation of Labour Unions at Tokyo YMCA. Then came the Association for Study of Socialism which later became the Social Democratic Party.

The recurring point Asian Christians made regarding matters of service was the need for coordination and cooperation among the service agencies of the different denominations, and even ecumenical service bodies in particular countries. There could be scandalous competition on their part in wanting to reach out with demonstrations in deeds of love for those in need. Alongside the consultations in Asia on new forms of service, there were similar discussions on joint action for mission. The challenge of the historical situation prompted Asian churchmen to reappraise, as mentioned earlier, the role of Christian service institutions, while the state in many countries jealously sought to exercise its responsibility for the promotion of welfare of the total national community.

Socialist-oriented critique of the service efforts of the churches in Asia was of tremendous help in crystallizing anew the basis and purpose of that service task of the church. The criticism levelled at the church in its ministry to those in need had to do with the view that these needy people, instead of being reinstated as persons who could assert their own personhood and right to life and dignity, were being turned into objects of charity – the shameful survival of an exploiting society. Hence to organize to distribute clothing to the naked, or to provide alms of food for the hungry was to patronize them and to indulge in wrong and condescending remedies. The need was to analyze the nature of a society which produces hunger and nakedness, and to renew or transform that society for justice and social security. Thus the churches in Asia were challenged to re-examine their traditional service concepts associated with personal and collective piety and to walk the second mile of prophetic diakonia.

Accordingly some new emphases were emerging for Asian churches. Diakonia was not to be understood and practised only in terms of merely helping members of the believing community. It was not to be the action of introverts, but to reach out in love to those beyond the members of the household of faith. As Dr W. A. Visser 't Hooft said: "By organizing the diaconal task on a worldwide basis, the ecumenical movement made it clear that it did not only believe in the solidarity of all Christians but also in solidarity with all who suffer from want."

Further it was not a matter of throwing occasional sops or a few crumbs of charity from the patrons to the miserable and the wretched. The emphasis was on the whole church reaching out to the whole person in the whole society. In the statements of the EACC this also meant involvement of the total Christian community made up of full-time service personnel as well as the individual members in their different walks of life. There was special attention given to affirm the lay apostolate. Formerly the so-called church-lay people who were Christian employees and executives in the church-related service institutions were almost a group set apart from those Christians who were exercising their Christian vocation in their various walks of life in society at large.

Mutual sharing of understandings about the biblical basis of service and exchange of experience out of concrete situations enriched the EACC in its ministry, as the regional ecumenical body formally started its life in 1959. Dr Visser 't Hooft and

Bishop Lesslie Newbigin were invited to initiate then the Mott Memorial Lectures series together with D. T. Niles. The role of the churches in Asia, along with the rest of the world Christian community, was examined in these lectures. When the programme of service was proposed within the EACC the distinctive Asian approach was to combine service with mission! The committee in charge of this programme itself was consciously named "The Committee on Inter-Church Aid for *Mission and Service*". In defining the functions of this committee the EACC Inaugural Assembly began with reference to the total commission of Christ. It went on to say:

> This total commission is given to the whole body of Christ's people everywhere, and involves them in many kinds of ministry or diakonia both within the worldwide fellowship of the church and in relation to those outside. But the varieties of ministry or services in the church are unified by the common concern of the church everywhere for mission – not its own, but its Lord's.[3]

The traditional Western approach to service had its own *raison d'être*. A proposal to combine concerns for service and mission in a single committee would probably have excited long debates and policy questions. Perhaps this Asian decision was the harbinger of the late WCC-IMC discussions at St Albans, and Herrenalb, and even the integration of WCC and IMC, which took place at the New Delhi Assembly in 1961.

The inspiration given by the task of service on a worldwide basis during this period of historical change in Asia challenged Asian Christians not only to be receivers, but also sharers of what they had. It is not because of their prosperity but in spite of their poverty that Asian churches count it a joy and privilege to participate in "confession in sharing action".

In the formative days of the EACC a response was given to a suggestion by the late Dr J. Leimena, then a minister in the Indonesian Cabinet, regarding possible action by the churches to meet the problem of food shortage in his nation. He mentioned it to me on my visit to Djakarta, and wondered whether the Christian community in Burma (a rice-surplus country) could supplement the government-to-government plan to provide rice from Burma to Indonesia. The bilateral state initiative was on a commercial basis. The response on the part of the churches was in terms of fraternal aid. The new experience I had was the surprising response

---

[3] *Witnesses Together*, official report of the Inaugural Assembly of the East Asian Christian Conference, Kuala Lumpur, 14–24 May 1959.

of congregations in remote parts of Burma to offer bundles of rice to be forwarded to Indonesia. Had we been approached for funds we would have been hard put to it. But *rice* could be shared by any average Burmese family! With resources augmented through WCC Inter-Church Aid, soon a shipment of rice was on its way from Rangoon to Djakarta. It was a new ecumenical experience with other later parallels among Asian churches. It could not have happened on that scale without WCC Inter-Church Aid. Such humble participatory experiences of Asian churches may not occupy much space, if at all, in reports at the world level. But what the instrumentality of inter-church aid had done to the spirit and mind of even remote rural village congregations cannot be adequately expressed.

As such a heart-warming and inspiring story comes to mind as we commemorate the fortieth anniversary of CICARWS, there is also a troubling memory. Working out of Burma (Rangoon) as regional ecumenical staff, I was made aware of a similar rice shortage in neighbouring Bangladesh (East Pakistan then). Though another colleague held the inter-church aid portfolio in EACC, I became involved in the concern for sending rice shipments to Dacca (the main port of the country in need) as fast as we could manage. It was only about three days' run from Rangoon to Dacca by ship. If purchases could be made swiftly in Burma with ecumenical funds, and formal processes followed promptly, I believed that relief action could have been taken to meet the need within a short time. But it turned out that rice from a distant part of the world was offered on payment of shipping fees (which alone possibly came to more than the cost of the commodity as well as that of the short distance shipping between next-door neighbours). Surely there possibly were larger considerations which a greenhorn from Asia, then, was unaware of!

The need for comparing notes and coordinating efforts between the regional and the world ecumenical bodies with their larger constituent members led to the periodical clarification of working relationships. Such understandings are incorporated into the relevant rules and procedures of the Christian Conference of Asia, as the EACC became. That Conference adopted this significant statement in 1975:

> In the interests of the total work of the church in each country in Asia, we appeal not only to the mission agencies, but also to the service agencies of the churches in other parts of the world, to give priority to programmes and actions expressing the common mind of all the churches in the area. It is our conviction that such agencies, many of which have large material resources, can unintentionally do great

damage to the Christian cause by supporting projects on a basis of unilateral consultation only. We urge that such agencies also undertake work in Asia only after full ecumenical consultation. Neither is it advisable that churches in Asia should make unilateral approaches to such agencies without full consultation with neighbouring churches.

Regarding emergency aid and service to refugees a statement arising out of the consultation held at Nassapur, India, soon after the coming together of Asian churches in regional fellowship, said:

> The value of worldwide emergency aid in times of crises or disasters is universally recognized. The participation of Asian churches in such giving should be increased.
>
> High priority should still be given to programmes devoted to the service of refugees. Great care should be taken however to ensure that the primary emphasis be put on service devoted to assisting the refugees to finding an entrance into a self-supporting way of life, rather than the provision of day-to-day sustenance.
>
> "Poor relief" type of feeding programmes should be entirely abandoned except for very brief emergency periods. The distribution of health-giving foods through hospitals, schools and orphanages should be continued under rigidly controlled conditions. . .

Such expressions of churches from a part of the world where emergencies, disasters and refugee problems are of near regularity of occurrence have contributed towards the development of ecumenical policies at the world level where insights from grass roots situations are always of great significance.

The programme of inter-church aid which emerged in connection with one of the most serious tragedies that overtook Asia demonstrated the instrumentality of WCC Inter-Church Aid in enabling the Asian churches to manifest their concern for their neighbours. As Vietnam Christian Service was the expression of concern on the part of American churches for people of Vietnam, Asian Christian Service became, in the early stages, the channel to minister to the needs of the Vietnamese, Laotians and Kampucheans in their tragic and unprecedented suffering. Asian Christian Service could not have been launched in the way it was without the existing relationships of trust and open sharing between Asian churches together and WCC Inter-Church Aid. The fact that concern could be expressed and service rendered among all the Indochina states, even during the height of tension among different sections of them, was evidence of the variety yet unity of perspectives and concerns which went to mould Asian Christian Service in its formative stage. Its thrust was not only directed towards the relief of the suffering, but also to contributing towards reduction of tensions among the contending sectors. Its ecumenical teams were given a hearing by crucial personalities in the conflict, and when critical war conditions overtook some places where Asian Christian Service volunteers were rendering service, they were reportedly spared undue hardships, presumably in recognition of the purpose for which they were understood to be present in danger zones. One cannot overestimate the significance of such humble attempts in the face of earth-shaking catastrophes. The victims of war and the displaced people were living proof and token of the tremendous social dislocation of not merely individuals but multitudes in the whole of Asia and the world at large.

I often repeat the telling words of the late Mr Ashok Mehta, the then minister of planning in India. He referred to the *world's final proletariat*, some 900 million people who were among the very neediest in the world. He said:

> There is no question of charity. There is a question of helping them with tools, with techniques, with possibilities whereby they may be able to produce much more. . . There are two difficulties. One is to create among them a sense of hope, of confidence, of purpose. . . Secondly, we need enough men and women of good will who feel that this is perhaps one of the most important tasks with which we must identify ourselves . . . reclaiming 900 million people of the world who are today in a state of abject depression. This *human reclamation*, requiring a peculiar type of social engineering, is to my mind the big challenge that all men of religion, all men of God, have to face. . . And if it is the proud claim of the Christian churches that they have spiritual understanding, spiritual agony, and spiritual outflow, then this has to be proved in the crucible of life itself. If it is the claim of our Christians that even to this day they feel the agony of Christ on the cross whenever humanity suffers, as it were, it has to be proved in action, not by any kind of statement. . .

It is relevant to follow this deep challenge for *human reclamation* with the sensitive expression of the late UN secretary-general U Thant when he articulated the need of global strategy for development after reciting the list of problems the developing nations faced:

> Our plans to meet these fundamental challenges are fragmentary and our resources, both human and material, pitifully inadequate, and meanwhile the clock ticks inexorably on. These are problems which never present the kind of dramatic ultimatum that questions of peace and war present. They slowly build up their crushing weight of misery until it becomes an overwhelming human tragedy. Can we not make the effort to advance out of our own sense of responsibility and knowledge, rather than be driven like refugees before the storm which may be unleashed by our inability to take hold of the future?

Ashok Mehta spoke of the challenge of *human reclamation* as he referred to the then 900 million *final proletariat* of the world. U Thant referred to the *development* problems of the global society.

Paul in his letter to the Galatians addressed them as "little children" and spoke of his travail "until Christ be formed" in them (Gal. 4:19). He was warning them of the danger of returning to the bondage of mere outward religion and the danger of becoming the children of Abraham *after the flesh* instead of children of *promise*. Christian service divorced from the concern for justice, human reclamation and renewal reveals that we are "babes" in Christian formation. But Christian service which is response to Christ in his incarnation, ministry, suffering, death and resurrection, reflects the travail for "Christ formation" in humanity that Paul was talking about. Adapting the thought of Ashok Mehta, the task of inter-church aid is for the restoration of the image of the Son in humanity, individually and corporately. WCC Inter-Church Aid had moved from relief reconstruction, mutual assistance within the family, to service of humanity at large and the crossing of frontiers to meet the challenges of society with compassion, hope, concern for justice and action for development.

The gathering task, the task of *human reclamation*, and prophetic ministry to bring human beings and communities nearer to the purpose of God, form the crucial content of the inter-church aid programme. The last chapter of the last book in the Bible tells of the river of life flowing from the throne of God and of the Lamb, with the tree of life on either bank bearing fruit every month and having leaves for the healing of the nations. And there is the assurance that God who had begun a good work in the WCC Inter-Church Aid will bring it to completion by the Day of Christ Jesus.

Africa

Samuel H. Amissah

Mr Samuel Amissah, who was general secretary of the All Africa Confer-
ence of Churches from 1964 to 1971, describes how the concept of inter-
church aid has come to life in situations as diverse and testing as the
Nigeria-Biafra conflict and the Sahelian drought. He tells, too, how that
concept has become rooted in African churches.

★ ★ ★

In his annual report for 1984 the general secretary of the Christian Council of Ghana, the Rev. A. K. Zormelo, paid the following
tribute:

> The Council would like to put on record the concern of all the
> churches in their contribution towards the solution of the drought and
> famine problem facing Ghana, and to show much appreciation for
> the role of the World Council of Churches in helping to solve these
> problems.

The tribute to the role of the World Council of Churches could
be echoed by many individuals and organizations in this country
and elsewhere in Africa who had received help in extremely critical
situations. The year 1983 had been particularly difficult for
Ghanaians. Two consecutive years of severe drought had resulted
in poor harvests; bushfires had destroyed large areas of food and
cash crops; the operating water level of the Akosombo Dam had
sharply fallen, resulting in countrywide rationing of electricity and
the suspension of the Volta Lake transportation. And, as if that
was not trouble enough, Nigeria had expelled about one million
illegal Ghanaian immigrants who over a few years had fled their
homeland to seek less harsh economic conditions abroad. Their
enforced return within a period of three months compounded the
problem of famine in Ghana. The local churches had rallied,
sharing what they had with the returnees. Later they turned their
attention to the acute feeding conditions in the prisons here and
there in the country where the death toll was mounting daily. In
response to appeals the international community gave generous

help in money and in kind, and the World Council of Churches played a magnificent role, seconding an experienced relief officer to the staff of the Christian Council to help in its relief work – receiving, storing and distributing the gifts of the churches abroad.

As I reflected on the report of the general secretary of the Christian Council against the background of Ghana 1985, my mind went back to the meeting of the WCC's Central Committee at Enugu, Nigeria, in 1965 and I was greatly cheered that what was started there had taken root and grown in stature, linking the churches of Africa and of the world together in a vigorous effort to meet human need. There could be no truer witness to the compassion of the Lord who challenged and commissioned his disciples by saying "Give them to eat" (Matt. 14:16), and "Feed my lambs" (John 21:15).

The Central Committee of the WCC was meeting in Enugu with Sir Francis Ibiam (as he then was), governor of Eastern Nigeria and a president of the World Council of Churches, playing host. I attended the meetings in my capacity as general secretary of the All Africa Conference of Churches (AACC), having been appointed at the First Assembly at Kampala, Uganda, in April 1963 and having assumed duty in Kitwe, Zambia, in January 1964. Several years before Enugu two leading personalities of WCC, Sir Hugh Foot (later Lord Caradon) and the late Dr Z. K. Matthews, had toured Africa discussing with churches and governments development programmes and the emerging problem of refugees. Already the WCC had been involved responding to ad hoc appeals for help. The upshot of the discussions in Africa and in the WCC was that the new infant organization, AACC, might be invited to' take over the responsibility for the involvement of the churches in the development programmes and the refugee problems of the emerging independent states of Africa. The Enugu meeting agreed to the proposal.

The General Committee of the AACC later accepted the proposal because it was covered by its mandate. When the churches of Africa met together for the first time in 1958 in Ibadan, Nigeria, they saw in the granting of independence by Britain to Ghana in 1957 the dawn of a new era for Africa; therefore, part of the message from Ibadan to the churches read:

> The continent of Africa will see unparalleled events and changes during the rest of this century, welcomed by some, feared by others. We pray that the Christian Church of Africa will play its role as champion, teacher, counsellor and shepherd during the crucial years.

If the church was to be a true shepherd, it could not shrink from involvement in any effort to ensure the welfare of the people. Accordingly the AACC agreed to launch an Ecumenical Programme for Emergency Action in Africa (EPEAA) which would seek to raise ten million dollars in five years to enable the churches to help in development programmes and refugee problems in Africa. An agency was set up on which the AACC and WCC were represented with some donor agencies as consultants and responsible to the General Committee of the AACC. The director was Dr Clinton Marsh of the United Presbyterian Church in the USA; he had helped to organize the First Assembly of the AACC in 1963, and he gladly accepted the invitation to return to Africa and help run the agency. Another key person was Kodwo Ankrah of the Methodist Church of Ghana who was on the staff of the Christian Council of Ghana; he was appointed refugee secretary. The agency operated from its own office separate from the AACC secretariat and kept in close touch with the churches of the AACC. It helped to formulate their projects and to present them for funding by the member churches of WCC and other donor bodies. When the agency wound up its affairs at the end of five years, AACC itself took over and refugee service became an integral part of its operation.

Over the period of the life of EPEAA the churches of Africa and outside were led into a deeper understanding of what it means to offer and receive aid; in fact the continuing learning process has deepened the fellowship among the churches and fostered a sense of the oneness of the church of Christ. Some of the lessons have been painful but effective, and it has meant speaking the truth in love. I recall the excitement of the first meeting of the agency held in Nairobi, Kenya, which gave time to discussing the raising and administering of funds. It was proposed that all grants to EPEAA should be unearmarked, leaving it to the judgment of the agency committee to determine priorities of need and the measure of help to be given; this proposal had the full backing of the African members of the meeting. One of the donor consultants promptly intervened by saying: "You cannot raise funds on that basis because those who contribute funds would want to specify what projects their funds must support." We who had supported the proposal of unearmarked grants gave in at that point, but continued to press the idea now and again not only in the work of the agency but also in the context of the total work of the AACC.

Our contention was that the giving of aid should not be a means of exercising pressure on those who benefit from the aid or those who administer it; there should be a basis of trust that those who receive and administer funds would be faithful stewards of the gifts to God's children in their need. If, however, trust was abused, then necessary corrective measures could justifiably be taken. It was interesting that in the process of time some of the funds for the agency and the AACC were given unearmarked, thus giving greater flexibility to the response to some needs. Towards the end of my term as general secretary of AACC an unsolicited grant of US$183,000 arrived from the USA to be used at the discretion of the AACC. It was in a way a tribute to the credibility of the AACC, a measure of the confidence that it had inspired among its donors. The big lesson was that trust generated by faithful stewardship is a necessary ingredient in effective inter-church aid operation.

I also recall a long night session of the General Committee of the AACC in Abidjan, Ivory Coast, during the Second Assembly of the AACC in 1969. The Nigeria-Biafra conflict was raging and AACC had member churches on both sides. The General Committee had to give guidance about action to be taken by the Assembly. Opinion was divided between issuing a statement and sending a goodwill mission. In the end the Assembly decided to send a mission which visited first Biafra and then Nigeria. It was led by the late William Tolbert, then vice president of Liberia and president of the World Baptist Alliance, and the members were: the Most Rev. John Kodwo Amissah (Catholic archbishop of Cape Coast, Ghana), the Rev. Seth Nomenyo of the Evangelical Church of Togo, the Rev. John Gatu (general secretary of the Presbyterian Church of East Africa), the Rev. James S. Lawson (associate general secretary of AACC) and the writer (general secretary of AACC). We flew into Biafra from Libreville, Gabon, by one of the "mercy-flights" which carried food and medicine. When we met Colonel Ojukwu and his senior officers we had a three-hour session at the end of which we joined hands standing in a circle and vice president Tolbert led us in prayer. Then Colonel Ojukwu said: "Because you have taken grave risks to come to us like this, I am prepared to talk to my brother Gowon without any pre-conditions." Later in Lagos, Nigeria, after a three-hour session with General Gowon which ended with prayer he said without any prompting: "I am prepared to talk with Ojukwu without any pre-conditions because the churches of Africa have sent you to me in this way."

About two weeks after the meetings in Biafra and Nigeria the members of the goodwill mission and representatives of the churches of Nigeria and Biafra met in Lomé, Togo, for a long weekend discussion about reconciliation and the president of Togo was most helpful in the arrangements for the meeting – accommodation, hospitality, transportation, security and funds. The reunion of friends on the first night was a deep emotional experience for all of us. They had not met since the beginning of the war and there was embracing of one another, vigorous handshaking, peals of hearty laughter and a bubbling over of conversation. The Spirit was moving among us and it stayed with us throughout the weekend; our prayers had been answered beyond our expectation. On the Sunday morning all the participants joined in worship at a church and as our names were called one by one during the introductions, we stood up to greet the congregation. They were spellbound to see people from Nigeria and Biafra sitting side by side, joining in worship. At the close of the service the members of the congregation fell over one another to shake hands with us and to wish us well in our deliberations. One of them, a senior civil servant, made a handsome donation towards the expenses of the mission. Earlier president Tubman of Liberia had sent us two thousand dollars through vice president Tolbert, and the Pope also had sent us two and a half thousand dollars through archbishop Amissah. The bulk of the expenses was under-written by the World Council of Churches.

On the same Sunday afternoon the members of the goodwill mission and their guests from Nigeria and Biafra attended a reception by the president of Togo in honour of the secretary-general of the United Nations, the late U Thant, who was visiting Togo. It was at the reception that the news flashed that the Nigeria-Biafra conflict had ended. It was significant that the discussions of the goodwill mission continued as planned to the Monday night. On the Tuesday morning the representatives of Biafra proceeded to Lagos at the invitation of the Christian Council of Nigeria; they went with two members of the mission to help in any way necessary.

We realized from our experience of the goodwill mission how vital it is to attempt to deal with the root causes of situations which led to human suffering and the giving of aid. We also realized that in the effort to deal with root causes, personal contact, sympathetic understanding, patient listening and courageous challenge based on our understanding of the gospel are essential to any meaningful intervention. Solidarity with those in need shown by standing alongside them or giving material aid of food, clothing, medicine or money generates strength and satisfaction shared by those who receive aid and those who give it. We realized further that the initiative to help inspires help from other sources, that goodwill multiplies and yields a richer harvest of love.

About five years after the Nigeria-Biafra experience there was another challenging experience of inter-church aid arising out of the Sahel situation where six West African countries bordering the Sahara were suffering from a six-year drought with a heavy toll of human and animal life. In April 1974 the WCC and the AACC jointly sponsored a seminar in Lomé, Togo, to discuss what might be done to help the victims of the drought in the short and in the long term. Apart from delegates from the stricken countries there were representatives from the UN, non-governmental organizations and churches in Europe, North America, and West Africa. One or two of us attended the seminar from Ghana.

In the deliberations it came out that some countries and organizations had already been involved in projects to help. When the question was asked: "What have the churches in West Africa been doing to help?" we were greatly embarrassed; the answer was "nothing". In fact some of us were hearing about the Sahel situation for the first time. Though we were close to the scene lack of information and communication had been a great stumbling block. On our return to Ghana we shared the information about the seminar with the churches, and as a result the Christian Council launched an appeal for help for the victims of the drought and raised about twelve thousand Ghana cedis. The Ghana Chaplains Association pledged to raise one thousand cedis. When the pupils of a secondary school heard the story of the drought, they without any prompting by their teachers decided to reduce one or two of their meals and thus raised two hundred cedis for the appeal.

The Methodist Church of Ghana, later reflecting on the Sahel situation and the response to the Christian Council appeal for help, became convinced of the need for a voluntary association in the country which would help people to hear about and respond quickly to emergency situations outside its borders which were causing great suffering. Accordingly an ad hoc committee was set up to look into the possibility of starting such an association. As a result of the efforts of the ad hoc committee the Ghana Association for Human Need came into being on 25 February 1978, almost four years after the Lomé seminar. The launching was performed by the Commissioner for Labour and Social Welfare of the government of Ghana and the special guests included church leaders from Togo and Miss Violet Gumbleton, a staff member of the World Council of Churches team based in Ouagadougou, Upper Volta, and looking after the projects in connection with the Sahel, who spoke about her work. Shortly after the launching I was invited as chairman of the Association to address the Synod of the Evangelical Church of Togo about the Association. It was a welcome opportunity to share with a sister country the efforts being made in Ghana to reach out to human need outside its borders.

In his inauguration address the Commissioner for Labour and Social Welfare underlined the need to offer aid as widely as possible:

> Whatever we do to help our own people should not blind us to the obligation to reach out to people elsewhere in their need. We are members not only of our families and our immediate society, but also part of the larger human family which is not bounded by countries but rather incorporates all of us everywhere. Whatever compassion, whatever sympathy, whatever concern we cherish should be for every human being as a person, and we should be ready to help according to our means.

It is interesting that the membership of the Association grew rapidly to include not only individuals but also the following bodies.

Girls Brigade
The University of Ghana
Anglican Young People's Association
Young Men's Christian Association
Christian Council of Ghana
Moslem Representative Council
Anglican Mothers Union
Ghana National Moslem Women's Association
Home Bible Students of the Ghana Mennonite Church
Ghana Industrial and Commercial Complex Limited
Divine Healing and Miracle Ministry Life
Methodist Women's Fellowship
Calvary Methodist Church
The Methodist Church, Ghana
Salvation Army, Ghana Territory
Evangelical Presbyterian Church
Salvation Church
Helping Hand Ladies Association

Through its diverse membership and work the Association is fostering a sense of inter-relatedness and concern for one another in a world of much human suffering and need, but also of great potential for sharing resources.

For some time we had tended to think of aid as a one-way traffic proceeding from the affluent churches, organizations and individuals of the industrialized countries to the poor, needy people of the world. Latterly it has dawned on us that aid is a two-way traffic, involving giving and receiving by all concerned. Thus "no church is too rich only to give, or too poor only to receive". Each has something to contribute out of its beauty or poverty for the enrichment of others. The gifts of God to individuals and groups are varied and everyone has something uniquely personal to share. It is in giving and receiving that we are truly enriched and that respect and love are deepened and our gratitude to the Great Giver of all we enjoy is enhanced.

The challenge of Enugu 1965 accepted by the AACC has yielded great dividends in many countries and churches of Africa, thanks to the supporting role of CICARWS.

Middle East

Archbishop Athanasios

In this chapter Archbishop Athanasios of the Coptic Orthodox Church in Egypt shows how the work of inter-church aid in the Middle East has expanded from great (and continuing) concern for the Palestinian refugees to work involving a wide spectrum of churches, many of them ancient, throughout the Middle East. He stresses not only involvement in development work, but the growth of ecumenical fellowship through inter-church aid.

★ ★ ★

Inter-Church Aid seems to have been one of the most powerful arms of the WCC in generating ecumenical activity among the churches of the Middle East. This does not mean that Inter-Church Aid always had more effect on churches than theology or ethics which are the concern of other sub-units of the Council. It is due more to the effectiveness of expanding Inter-Church Aid activities among the local communities and the leadership of the various churches.

I will divide this article into three sections: firstly, "coming together", an historical appraisal of the nature of Inter-Church Aid involvement in the beginnings of ecumenical activities among the churches of the Middle East; secondly, "working together", an assessment of the ways in which the work of Inter-Church Aid has contributed to human development among the nations of the Middle East; thirdly, "growing together", the nature of the growth in understanding and ecumenicity between the donor and recipient churches.

Coming together

In August 1948 the newly-created International Christian Committee based in East Jerusalem dispatched two cables to the Inaugural Assembly of the WCC requesting relief supplies and asking the Assembly to "examine [the] Palestine problem in light of principles of Christian justice with the view to recommend rectification of obvious wrongs. . ."

In 1950, the Central Committee of the WCC meeting in Toronto declared in a statement on refugees:

> The Central Committee remembers with deep sympathy the continued sufferings of the Arab refugees in the Middle East. It calls on the churches to keep this urgent human need before their members. It asks the Department of Inter-Church Aid and Service to Refugees to explore in what ways the churches and other voluntary agencies may give more effective help, in cooperation with the United Nations Relief and Works Agency, for the relief of the refugees and their ultimate rehabilitation.

Ever since, the issue of the Palestinian refugees has been a burning one. Ecumenical assistance through the WCC for these people has grown from one thousand pounds sterling in 1948 to 2.7 million dollars in 1984.

The Near East Christian Council (NECC) requested the WCC, together with the International Missionary Council (IMC) to convene a conference of Christian leaders to study the problem of the Palestinian refugees. Responsibility for this was assigned to the WCC's Department of Inter-Church Aid and the meeting was held in Beirut in May 1951. A second conference was also held in Beirut in May 1956.

At a consultation with representatives of North American churches in New Haven, USA, July 1957, Leslie Cooke, then director of Inter-Church Aid, pointed out that the department (of Inter-Church Aid) "is concerned both to channel support to the NECC (for refugee work) and to develop closer contacts with the Eastern churches which are outside the membership of that Council".

The project list for the first time included grants to Orthodox bodies in Jordan, Lebanon and Iraq in 1958. In 1961 there was a project of the Coptic Orthodox Church in Egypt and since then projects for Episcopalians, Protestants, Eastern Orthodox, Oriental Orthodox, Assyrian and Chaldean churches have been on the list.

Among the six addresses to the world consultation on inter-church aid held in Swanwick, England, in July 1966 there was the "urgency of a common diakonia in the churches" by Metropolitan Emilianos Timiadis, which was extremely valuable, and among the six "situation sessions" was one on "Europe and Orthodox Countries and the Middle East", again of outstanding quality. There were fifteen representatives from the churches of the Middle East; those of Egypt were represented by Mr Assad A. E. Moutigalli Assaad of the Evangelical Church, Fr Xavier Eid of the Greek Catholic Church, and the writer, of the Coptic Orthodox Church.

At this time, the only regional coordinating body of the churches in the region was the Near East Council of Churches (earlier the Near East Christian Council) whose members were Evangelical and Episcopal churches.

The year 1965 marks a turning point in the history of inter-church aid work in the Middle East. After several negotiations between the NECC, the Near East Committee on Inter-Church Aid, and Mr M. C. King, then the DICARWS secretary for Orthodox churches and countries and the Middle East, the Executive Committee of DICARWS in its May meeting authorized the director:

a) to create committees responsible for recommending to the division regular inter-church aid projects originating with the churches and Christian organizations in (1) Syria and Lebanon, and (2) in Jordan, and generally assist the division in inter-church aid in these countries;

b) to invite appropriate church men in the countries concerned to be members of these committees and to lay down terms of reference and constitutions for these committees; and

c) to take the necessary steps for the appropriate transference of functions, residual funds, etc. from the existing Near East Committee on Inter-Church Aid to the new committees.

These two committees were formed immediately afterwards. Along with them was an Ecumenical Advisory Council in Egypt including Coptic Orthodox, Coptic Evangelical, Greek Orthodox and Greek Catholics playing the role of a counterpart of DICARWS in Egypt.

In 1972 CICARWS convened a consultation in Salamis, Cyprus, to decide on general directives for inter-church aid work in the Middle East.

An important milestone in the ecumenical movement in the Middle East came when the Orthodox churches were voted into full membership of the Near East Ecumenical Committee for Palestine Refugee Work. This led to the movement towards a more representative regional ecumenical body, culminating in the establishment of the Middle East Council of Churches (MECC) in 1974. The Orthodox, Evangelical and Episcopal churches became members of this new regional body. This does not mean that they did not work together earlier. The Salamis consultation is a witness to the fact that the churches represented in these committees worked hand in hand in inter-church aid and with CICARWS.

Working together

Within the field of inter-church aid the churches worked together and came closer. Members of the same family – like the Coptic Orthodox, Armenian Apostolic and Syrian Orthodox churches which have the same understanding of the faith and belong to the same Oriental Orthodox family – witness that through the WCC and the common activities within inter-church aid they came to know each other better.

CICARWS has helped communities of the Middle East, Christian and non-Christian alike. Some examples have been village development projects in Greece, poultry and livestock projects in Turkey, and a massive reafforestation programme in Algeria. Assistance has also been given following earthquakes in Algeria and Morocco and more recently in Lebanon for rehabilitation and reconstruction.

The screening process of projects has developed over the years. At first projects went through local committees. Sometimes churches commented on them but in most cases they were sent directly to CICARWS and the screening was done in Geneva. Gradually there came into being the regional screening group in which half of the members were chosen by the churches of the area and the other half chosen by CICARWS. Now the regional group is not only concerned with screening projects but also in wider sharing issues and exchange of ecumenical visits.

It is progress that critical decisions on projects have moved from Geneva to the regional screening group. In some countries there is now national pre-screening. In the first phase people learned that programmes should take priority over buildings. The projects at first were more ecclesiastical, like church buildings, theological schools and salaries for priests. In the second phase, project emphasis shifted to community centres, retreat centres, youth camps, projects of village service, pastoral activity, women's activities and Christian education. In the third phase, there was emphasis on development in livestock, vocational training, leadership training, loan funds, land reclamation, integrated village development and concern for people living in slums. Decision-making became more or less the responsibility of the project carriers in projects which were part of "country programmes" such as the Department on Service to Palestine Refugees and the Emergency Relief and Rehabilitation Appeal for Lebanon.

More recently there have been consultations involving visitation and discussion of rural development in the framework of ecumenical sharing. Christian and Muslim rural experts from Turkey, Egypt, Lebanon, the West Bank, Gaza and Geneva were present at the meetings held in Tunisia in 1982 and Egypt, in 1984.

These rural sharing meetings have shown how CICARWS helps to encourage cooperation between experts of different religious backgrounds working on common problems.

Growing together

In November 1984 a consortium was held in Cairo to draw up a nationwide church programme for the Coptic Orthodox Church. Participants were from that Church and from overseas partner agencies.

It was significant also that Bishop Ireneos of Chania, Crete, who is involved in development work in Crete, visited Egypt for the first time in his life and attended a meeting in the Evangelical Centre in Itsa, Minya, together with other Christians and Muslims. They went to Beni Suef and visited the writer and some of the development projects in his diocese: the Coptic diakonia centre, which includes youth clubs, a library, St Mary's Hall, offices, a leadership training centre for women development workers, and a museum and audiovisual aid department. The bishop also visited the women's centre and a hostel for university students and had lunch in the convent of the Daughters of Mary – the first and so far only convent for active sisters who have managed successfully to combine the life of monasticism and service. He showed great interest and enthusiasm for everything he visited and the people he met, their spirituality, the work of service in the diocese and especially the expression of their faith in service for their community.

Through CICARWS activities and visits of projects and their communities, many Western churches and local communities began to see and learn about churches in the Middle East. Publicity, collections for projects and news about activities in churches (e.g. women's organizations, the involvement of laity in service, pastoral care, Christian education and youth activities), helped people in the West to see that the responsibility of service lies in the hands of laity (women[1] and men) and not totally with the clergy. Many groups from Western churches came and visited, and for them the Middle East now is not only a Bible land, the land of antiquities, but a land of living churches. Many Westerners through experience gradually began to discover that the Orthodox

---

[1] On 23 December 1975 the Coptic Orthodox Church held a special day to recognize women's role in church and society on the occasion of the International Women's Year. The day was patronized by Pope Shenouda III. One of its features was the recommendation that women should represent the Coptic Orthodox Church at the regional and national levels ecumenically, sharing in policy and decision-making within the country.

liturgy has great meaning and significance for the lives of the faithful as expressed in service.

There is growth within the church. The number of deaconess and deacon community centres is increasing. The Order of the Daughters of St Mary in Beni Suef was established by the writer and blessed by the beloved Coptic Pope Kyrollos VI in 1966. Presently forty sisters are involved in a number of developmental and educational projects.

What Dr Visser 't Hooft said in Nairobi in 1975 is also significant: "Go to the western desert of Egypt and observe the immense development in the Monastery of St Makarios in Wadi Natrun."

Some churches of varying denominations have vocational training and development projects and are now working together in the same vicinity. An example of this is the latest step in negotiations between the Council of Catholic Bishops of Egypt and the MECC Cairo office whereby there are proposals for the Roman Catholic Church to join the MECC.

Finally, a very important step in growing together has been the realization on the part of project carriers of the effort and hardship involved in fund-raising and also learning about the actual procedure of raising funds. At the same time, fund-raising agencies are learning about the priorities of the project carriers and the changing situations which occur during the execution of the projects.

The educational programmes that these agencies go through to tell the people and official bodies about the various projects draw heavily on the clear description the carriers give to the projects, the way they are implemented and interpreted.

Although the trend has been to transfer decision-making more into the hands of the project carriers, the projects which often appeal to donors have to be people-oriented and of a community development nature, e.g. leadership training, vocational training and other ways that help people to develop their experience, their power of decision and their ability to work together and support their community.

The 1969 Cyprus consultation said: "All work must be done not only *for* the Palestinians but *with* them." This seems to be a rule for all human development projects.

Let me end by recalling what I said during the CICARWS Commission meeting in Sofia, Bulgaria, in 1973:

> CICARWS is fundamentally a socially-minded commission because it tries to take the money from the rich and give it to the poor and needy.

The members of CICARWS are loyal in a practical way to ecumenism and to humanity, for they work in three dimensions: horizontally we are Catholic, vertically we are Orthodox and at the base we are Evangelical.

Above: Some of the 21 million tree seedlings planted in Algeria following the war, early 1960s

Below: Families work together on community projects following the earthquake in Guatemala, 1976

Photos: Bachofen, WCC, Peter Solbjerghøj

Above: Distribution of much-needed relief goods in Poland, early 1980s

Right: Rebuilding homes after the earthquake in Skopje, Yugoslavia, 1963

Below: Transporting salt codfish in Biafra, 1968-69

Latin America

Marta Palma

Ms Marta Palma, of Chile, deeply involved in recent years in the work of the World Council's Commission on Inter-Church Aid, Refugee and World Service, gives here a vivid personal account of struggles in her own continent and the role of WCC Inter-Church Aid in them. World Council involvement in Latin America is more recent than involvement in other continents; it is certainly no less demanding.

★ ★ ★

The history of our peoples has been marked by the signs of domination and also by those of liberation.

One expression of that domination is the great inequality by which in every country a small group enjoys wealth and wellbeing while the vast majority suffer hunger and want.

In face of this, there has been an awakening of consciousness among the people, and various kinds of campaigns have been undertaken in order to change the structures of oppression. The ruling classes, in alliance with elements outside the region, have reacted by producing various counter-measures aimed at smothering any such efforts in search of sovereignty. Their response has been an authoritarianism based on military power and supported in recent years by the doctrine of national security. In the name of that security, repression and extreme violence have been employed against the people and their organizations. Meanwhile, the peoples continue their struggle and are devising more and more new and creative forms of resistance to the forces of death.

The churches have been uncertain whether to adopt a justifying or indifferent attitude towards the injustice of those in power, or to espouse the cause of the poor and oppressed in the name of a liberating Christianity. There is no doubt that in the course of our history the majority of them have adopted the first attitude, legitimizing domination and in many cases serving as its instruments. Nevertheless, in the last few decades in particular, a new consciousness has emerged in our churches, and they are increasingly committing themselves to the campaign for the advancement and defence of life. Numerous Christians have given their lives in this cause, and many in country and town bear anonymous witness to their faith by the side of the poor.

In this context the involvement of WCC Inter-Church Aid has assumed various forms in each particular situation. Its presence has been profoundly marked by the social and political conflicts affecting the region, by the history of the churches, and by the course taken by ecumenical activity as a whole, with its advances and withdrawals, successes and difficulties.

It is difficult to convey in a few pages the wealth and specific nature of its involvement in each particular situation. For that reason, while in no way denying its very real diversity, we shall present the work of WCC Inter-Church Aid in Latin America through various types of programmes by which this sub-unit supports churches and groups in a broad perspective of human rights, and in which other sub-units of the WCC are also involved. The Central American situation is reserved for separate examination, because of the special features presented by a region harassed by the threat of war.

Changing the signs of death into roads of life

In Latin America, violations of human rights are the result of a political logic and rationale, that is to say, the action of multinational capitalism which, in defence of its interests, opposes the aspirations of the poor peoples to construct just societies with effective respect for their rights.

The struggle of the oppressed peoples, therefore, is not a conflict of abstract forces, but a campaign to achieve their historical goals, and is expressed in concrete forms of practical action.

Actions on behalf of human rights supported by the churches and by men and women of goodwill have for many people come to constitute means of expression, occasions for joint action, for showing solidarity, and providing an opportunity for regrouping their organizations. In many cases they have led the churches to turn to the world of the poor by taking their distress to heart and recognizing them as brothers and sisters. In this way their witness has gained in credibility and prophetic force.

In this context, too, a new spirituality has been emerging, which finds expression in the liturgical life of some churches and in the new meaning that some signs and symbols have assumed as new ways of denouncing injustice and announcing the kingdom (fasting, pilgrimages, way of the cross, prayers, etc.).

At the same time the conception of human rights has widened, as laid down at the Itaicí meeting in Brazil, 1980, to include the fight for life on all levels. As already noted, Inter-Church Aid has supported activities on these lines in the region in close collaboration with the Human Rights Resources Office for Latin America and other WCC sub-units. A more comprehensive account of the work of this sub-unit in the region would have to mention that, in close collaboration with the churches and associated bodies, it has supported the following types of programmes, in some cases in conjunction with other WCC units and sub-units as well: pastoral work among the people; training of ecumenical personnel, development and social welfare workers; popular education; ecumenical and popular publications; aid to aboriginal and peasant groups; emergency relief and support to self-sufficiency schemes; aid to refugees and migrants; exchange of personnel.

The human rights campaign: a challenge to the Christian conscience

Cain, where is your brother?

The only thing I ask for is to know about my son, to know where he is, and for him to be given back to me. . . The only thing I am asking for is help to find him, for him to be given back to me, regardless.

This cry is often heard in our Latin America. There are thousands upon thousands of persons arrested by the forces of repression who now swell the lists of people detained and disappeared.

The long vigil by the Mothers of the Plaza de Mayo in Buenos Aires has become well known. These women, who risked their own lives in the days of the military dictatorship, are organized to seek their loved ones. With the coming to power of a democratic government in that country, a long investigation into the disappearances has begun.

The writer Ernesto Sábato, president of the National Commission on the Disappearance of Persons in that country, referred to this problem in a special TV programme as follows:

Our judgment is concerned with the ultimate values of the human condition, with the values which the great civilizations have always defended, which the great religions have postulated, which all right-minded and decent human beings have respected. And at this level we can say that all these principles have been appallingly violated. It is therefore a monstrous crime against humanity.

I believe that (what happened in Argentina) was the reign of the devil on earth. Devilish actions have been committed not only against persons presumed or really guilty of some crime, but against the immense majority of absolutely innocent people.

There is no doubt that this, like other forms of destruction of life, is a visible expression of the demoniacal forces unleashed against men, women and children with the aim of destroying the life and identity of the peoples. Nevertheless it is impressive to observe in the onward journey of these peoples how they are able to lift themselves up and, despite their wounds, transform these signs of death into signs of resurrection.

In Laja, a small village in southern Chile, nineteen corpses were found in a hidden grave dug by the military. They were the bodies of missing persons discovered there after six years of agonizing search. The following comment by the priest José Aldunate indicates these signs of resurrection emerging from this painful, traumatic experience. The thoughts arose as he accompanied the people flocking to the cemetery to bury their sacrificed children:

As I walked in the column I felt that with me the church was journeying with its people. This people which surrounded me was no doubt not identical with the parish congregation, but was the people to which the church should devote itself: the exploited, the oppressed, hungry and thirsty for justice (Matt. 5:1–12). There are circumstances in which I feel out of place, but here, on the contrary, as a churchman, I can identify myself fully with this people on the march and with its fundamental commitment. I perceived in their activities and expressions the action of the Spirit of God. I perceived that here and now falsehood was being overcome, justice done, life promoted. This people was responding to the inherent longing of humanity for a kingdom of life, justice and peace in which all would be brothers and sisters.

Here under the blue dome of the sky I felt I was witnessing a new declaration of human rights. It was not a matter mainly of civil rights, which in fact never were much of a solution for a people that has suffered and gone hungry since time immemorial. What was at stake was the fundamental human right to life. In face of the unpunished murder of its sons, and of its own moral destruction, Laja was reacting, and with sure instinct translating its protest into determination to fight on.

Two biblical events seemed to me to give this march its deep significance. The first was that of the Hebrew people in its exodus from Egypt to take possession of the land which God had given it. This too was a march of liberation. It was obvious that everyone felt this. . . They were literally dancing along, as the Hebrews did before the Ark in which God went with them. The second event was the entry of Jesus into Jerusalem in a spontaneous demonstration by the Jewish people – greeting Jesus the liberator. And when their shouts scandalized the temple priests, Jesus answered: "If these were silent, the very stones would cry out."

The cry "Where are our brothers and sisters?" has led many Christians in Latin America to discover just where they themselves stand as a people, and where Jesus is, the Lord of life who changes despair into liberating hope.

In this process, some have recognized themselves as forming part of that world of the poor (as in the case of some Pentecostal churches), while others have dedicated themselves in solidarity with them to the defence of their human rights.

Some churches or elements in them, in collaboration with non-ecclesiastical groups, are beginning to promote initiatives on the plane of direct action and prophetic denunciation. The mere will to do something is not enough, however; international solidarity is also needed, and backing from the ecumenical family.

In view of the seriousness and magnitude of the problem, and at the request of the churches in the region, the WCC in 1973 created the Human Rights Resources Office for Latin America. Various initiatives resulted from this joint commitment: solidarity organizations, human rights defence committees and others devoted to the difficult task of legal defence of victims of arbitrary arrest; anti-torture campaigns; care for political prisoners; assistance in the search for people detained and "disappeared"; aid to refugees and exiles; campaigns in defence of basic rights such as health, work, housing, education, etc.

On the basis of the practical work of these solidarity organizations and of the practical experience and reflection of the churches and the people's organizations, the problem of human rights has come to be restated in terms of collective rights, the rights of peoples, thus broadening a concept which had been too restricted to individual and political rights. The extension moves from individual to collective, from political to economic and to all spheres of everyday life where the right to life is at stake.

In recent years the human rights situation in the region has worsened. At the same time the churches' commitment has grown and strengthened. Through its Human Rights Resources Office, the WCC has attentively supported that involvement as well as the awakening of sympathetic understanding in other churches of Latin America and other regions of the world. At the same time concrete operations have continued to be carried out on the plane of making the facts known internationally and emergency relief. Some of this work has been undertaken in recent years in conjunction with CLAI (Latin American Council of Churches), a regional organization which has worked more particularly in the field of the churches' pastoral care and study.

In many countries of the region, human rights violations have become a permanent feature. As a result, human rights programmes themselves have assumed a permanent character within the general perspective of rebuilding a social fabric destroyed, or at least damaged, by the repression. These programmes usually include measures to obtain redress for individual injury as well as collective action on common problems, with educational work as an important element. Programmes of this type have been supported in recent years by WCC Inter-Church Aid and in particular by its Latin America Desk in conjunction with the Human Rights Resources Office.

The struggle for survival

As we noted above, one of the most serious and agonizing problems affecting our region is unemployment and underemployment with its consequent hunger and distress. In recent years this has prompted a revision and restatement of the approach to the basic needs of food, health, education, housing, which, when unsatisfied, destroy the identity and personality of individuals, groups and communities.

On the basis of the various practical experiences of people's groups and the churches, the need has been felt to act in solidarity with those who see their right to life endangered because they lack the elementary means of subsistence. Concrete actions of this kind have given rise to processes of organization and popular education in a general perspective of development. WCC Inter-Church Aid has supported some of these programmes in the region, as well as manifestations of solidarity that have sprung up spontaneously among the poor as forms of resistance.

The significance these experiences have had for those taking part in them is reflected in the following testimony of two squatters, who in conjunction with other families set up a soup kitchen to relieve their hunger.

> This kitchen is very important for us, because as well as serving to feed us it makes us realize that we can do things together. It also helps us to get to know one another and share our problems and organize. We realize that we are all out-of-work people with problems of housing, education for our children, health. This makes us feel stronger and we are growing together.

Another adds:

> Here we realize the solidarity there is between us poor people. My husband is out of work. My four sons have stopped attending school because we haven't any money to send them there. The poor little things have suffered a lot. My husband keeps pestering, but it does not get us anywhere. Here, I don't work only for my own family but for all. . .

From troubles shared spring signs of life which make them believe in the hope of a more decent life. Friendship, solidarity and the efforts of groups and organizations are multiplying in our Latin America, building an emerging culture of *life*, which redeems and gives value to everyday experiences, and are a good omen of a new society of brothers and sisters in the future, marked by justice.

Work with children in the world of the people

The children of the people's world are coming more and more to be one of the central concerns of the churches and popular organizations in Latin America. Gradually they have rid themselves of the over-simple idea that relief work is all that is needed with children. In Nicaragua, as part of building a new society, state schemes are being put into effect aimed at giving the child proper opportunities for growth and training. In socially and economically depressed situations, too, the child is an important character, and although children's problems are not taken over by the state, various solidarity organizations and development agencies are launching schemes with social construction in mind.

On the basis of these experiments, some of them supported by WCC Inter-Church Aid, the community has come to appreciate the possibility of concentrating its efforts on problems affecting children. Some countries have seen initiatives such as the creation of "children's rights committees" and others with similar aims.

The following experience might be met with in any of these countries, with similar features:

> It is Saturday. The day is fine. The children arrive smiling, and greet "uncle". He calls them, they gather round and sing. They decide what they are going to do, as they always do. This time they will talk about "fears". The small children will draw and the older ones will talk about what makes them afraid – night, hunger, punishment, the police. . .
>
> They learn by playing, and at the end of the afternoon there is a glass of milk and a piece of bread.

What is the world of these children like? Their fathers are generally out of work or have jobs which don't provide enough for them to live on. Their houses are small, with yards that are small too. They haven't proper space to live. Their world is poor in stimulus and experiences. No toys, no books. Often because of their parents' anxieties, produced by the problems they have to cope with, the children are subjected to authoritarian, aggressive treatment. They lack affection, protection, warmth, security.

It is hard to be a child in this world of poverty. Nevertheless children play in their groups in the streets of their town. They develop the ability to survive by selling sweets, cleaning cars.

How do young people join in? With jokes and serious moments, the young unemployed and some students devise and carry out schemes to build "freedom spaces" for children. Young people are awake to the problems of children, which remind them of their own childhood of poverty and make them think about it. This makes them more mature, they learn to get a better knowledge of children, of their community and of themselves. They learn to amuse themselves together, to be cheerful despite the problems.

How do parents join in? The only way to ensure that what the child has learnt lasts and has some impact on home and community, is by getting the parents involved; they discover their capacity for self-education; they discover how to bring up their children in freedom, better ways to survive, how to organize themselves and join in.

Theological training: theological accompaniment of the new practices

The processes of theological training based on the people's struggle, have also formed part of the work of WCC Inter-Church Aid in the region, especially in the last few years.

Backing for various programmes of pastoral work among the people and popular publications and communications contribute to this process, which seeks to study the faith on the basis of concrete problems of everyday life. These programmes have accompanied experiences of involvement, by both Catholic and Protestant groups, and assume various forms to match the characteristics of the various countries, and promote deeper commitment based on a Christian identity. In some cases they help to bring home to the churches the urgency of problems of want and injustice.

The following testimony reflects the process lived through by many of our Protestant brothers and sisters in the region. A Pentecostal brother is speaking:

> At first I was very traditionalist; my ideas of Christianity were pure spirituality. Then as I gradually assimilated the work my church was doing and the theological study guides, I came to realize that the work of the Christian is not solely inside the church. It was not easy, however; first of all I had a lot to learn, I had to face my own reality, find out a great deal, ask a lot of questions, before coming to understand the situation for myself. Gradually I drew my own conclusions, and in fact realized that I did not feel very happy about that traditional position in which one as it were regards those "outside", those of the

"world", as something alien to what is ours, as people who are rather worse than we are, to whom we feel rather superior. After a while I began to regard them as my equals.

The process led this brother to devote himself to the housing campaign, and he became leader of a community of over 10,000 people, 70 percent of them out of work.

Everyday practical life presents Christians with challenges and new situations which they have to cope with in the light of their faith. One of these is the problem of what methods to employ to win respect for their rights in authoritarian situations where there are no regular channels of citizen participation. He relates:

> We have urged non-violence, but I have come to realize that the time has come when dialogue is no longer enough, but a more militant, more aggressive action has to be taken, since dialogue alone has got us nothing but more dialogue and nothing concrete. . . For me as a Christian leader it is not easy, but at the same time I understand that not everything can be achieved without a fight.

Christians who engage in liberation work and prophetic denunciation are often accused of engaging in "political" activities, or of being "communists".

> Sometimes I talk with Protestant brothers and sisters who are alarmed when they learn that I too am a Protestant. "How can you be political?" they say. "You cannot be political, because God's word (the Bible) says we must not get involved in that." Then I answer: "Well, then, tell me where the Bible says I must not get involved in politics", and unfortunately, for I don't like to embarrass them, since that isn't quite the best thing to do, they haven't yet been able to show me where the Bible says that a Christian must not take part in anything. For if that's the difficulty, well then, we have Daniel's example. Daniel became a great statesman in Babylon; we also have the example of Joseph, who, we might say, was an economics minister more or less – the example of how he governed in Egypt, how rationing was organized to prevent food supplies running out. . .

Another sphere of concern for Christian thought and action is the problem of unity. This has shown, as was evident in Itaicí, too, that action in the name of justice creates new and valuable forms of rapprochement and collaboration between Christians and also with non-believers. This is what has been called grassroots ecumenism, which is built up in the daily struggle in defence of life for bread, work, housing, health. It takes place in the context of the struggle of the poor who by their dedication evangelize the church by awakening its awareness and impelling it to act in solidarity. This grassroots ecumenism has been springing up in

Catholic communities among the people, and also in some Protestant churches. A brother gives the following account:

> The first activity that I joined was a "homeless committee". It was important for me, because the other members were Catholics, and it was interesting for them to realize that among their comrades they had a Protestant, a fact that amazed them. Together we came to the conclusion that Protestants and Catholics had a lot in common; since we were brothers and sisters, we believe in the same God; we have some differences but there are many things on which we agree, and a lot of things to do and think about together, for example, concern to fight for those who suffer. . .

What is the ideal that inspires this action on behalf of life? A brother writes:

> As Christians we have to give an example, we have to be in front, showing the world that we don't fight only for the salvation of souls but also campaign for a better quality of human life here on earth; because Jesus said that the kingdom of heaven is among us, and God's will is that the kingdom should begin here and now. The kingdom is already coming to birth here and now, as we ourselves set about striving to help others to grow together; by that we shall be showing others the kingdom of God, not just in words but in deeds. It would be good if they were to say: "This Protestant preaches, but he also practises what he preaches."

Central America: the fight for life

I firmly believe that the revolutionary struggles of the peoples of Central America spring from the physical distress and social discrimination which are deepening day by day throughout Central America and the Caribbean. This is rooted in the profound imbalance and injustice on both the national and international level.

I firmly believe that the peoples of Central America have a right to be the builders of their own history.

(From the speech of Adolfo Pérez Esquivel, Nobel Peace Prizewinner, at the International Conference on Nicaragua and for Peace in Central America in 1984.)

The problem of every Central American country, a problem which has dragged on since the last century, has been that of sovereignty. To be sovereign for these peoples, as indeed for the rest of Latin America, means to decide their own destiny, build for themselves, without the destructive interference of outside interests. Yesterday, Central America was an agglomeration of "banana republics" run by the transnational fruit companies; today it is an important geopolitical area inside the Reagan administration's hegemony plan. At the present time security interests, that is to say the strategic military interests of the United States in the region, are more important than economic interests, although these no doubt play a far from negligible role.

In both cases there has been a need for governments subservient to these interests external to the region and to each of the countries in it. The most brutal example today is Honduras, which has practically been turned into a US military base. Furthermore, this logic has entailed suppression of any attempt at self-determination by these peoples. In this sense, Nicaragua represents the triumph of the dream of sovereignty and the failure of attempts to prevent it, and that is why they are seeking to destabilize it. The favourite pretext is the "communist threat", in a profoundly Christian country whose people do not even know what communism is, and the only thing they long for is decent living conditions.

Within these coordinates, Central America is a sub-continent in crisis. In every country there are people working to build up their nation into a truly sovereign state. In every country there are also sectors associated with ruling powers who deploy all their cruelty and contempt for the life of the poor in the service of the geopolitical strategy dominant in the region. This is seen most tragically in countries like Guatemala, or El Salvador, where for the last four years or so civil war has cost thousands upon thousands of victims, by murder not only of adults but also of innocent children, and by disappearance, torture and imprisonment.

The life of the churches is not untouched by this polarization. The struggle for liberation in Central America has challenged the Christian conscience, and inspired vital commitments, many ending in martyrdom – from that of nameless Christian peasant militants in Guatemala or El Salvador to that of a Catholic archbishop, Monsignor Romero.

However, support for the "establishment" has wide backing in the churches of the region and is reinforced by the whole tendency of people with vested interests in the region to be channels for the ideological spread of conservatism.

In the last few years the problem of refugees and migrants has become tragically acute. Thousands of families are fleeing from persecution and torture, and many of them escape death only by a miracle. They are driven to abandon their countries in search of ways of survival, in flight from hunger, fear and despair.

The WCC presence in the region

The WCC has constantly expressed special concern about the Central American area. The involvement of WCC Inter-Church Aid through various desks (Latin America Desk, Refugee Service, Personnel Secretariat, and others) has operated in close connection with other offices and sub-units, among which we should mention the Human Rights Resources Office for Latin America, the Commission on the Churches' Participation in Development and the Commission of the Churches on International Affairs. Close collaboration has been maintained with churches and ecumenical organizations of the countries and the region.

Without attempting to include all the forms which its relations with this area have assumed, we consider it essential to mention activities which have been given priority as joint undertakings:

1) emergency appeals for humanitarian relief in situations of conflict, and also in situations of reconstruction, as in Nicaragua;

2) attentive support through pastoral visits to the region in coordination with churches of other countries and with CLAI;

3) actions in various human rights fields particularly in defence and protection of life, in coordination with international and regional organizations both ecclesiastical and specialized;

4) actions in aid of refugees and migrants in cooperation with international organizations, churches and partner agencies;

5) circulation of information and evidence collected through churches of the area.

My experience in CICARWS: learning and sharing

My experience of about ten years in the ecumenical movement, especially in connection with CICARWS, has meant for me an incredible process of learning.

In the first place I have learnt from my brothers and sisters in Latin America, from their endeavours and hopes – from nameless men and women, squatters, peasants, unemployed, working women, working-class families; from children in whose eyes one reads a question about the future and sometimes uncertainty about an anxious present; from the love of young people, their efforts and determination to build a better world; from professional men and women and technicians who, though not of the people, have nevertheless devoted themselves to them and put their knowledge at the service of the most disinherited; from politicians and social leaders who with constant vigilance seek the best for their community, people or nation; from Christians who live their faith in Jesus Christ, and from the non-Christians who also live their faith in humankind and seek to transcend the limits of the present; in short, from the men and women of my continent, most of them anonymously merged in solidarity in all its shapes and forms.

During this ecumenical period I have learnt from many Christians of various parts of the world, who in their own particular circumstances are bearing witness to their faith and, although many of them live in rich countries, express solidarity with the suffering peoples and their churches. Often that commitment has meant they have had to face rejection and difficulties from other people. I have learnt the value of dialogue with persons from other backgrounds and with different positions, since distrust and lack of cooperation is often due to absence of dialogue and joint reflection.

From my Latin American continent I have come to know more closely how urgently human life is at stake. I have seen the deterioration in regard to human rights both in extreme situations and in respect of the living conditions in our countries, where men and women in many cases are reduced to despairing survival. I have also seen and learnt the strength of the solidarity among the poor, their creativity in overcoming the forces of death and in finding ways to battle on. I have also seen the support given by many churches, especially their hierarchies, to the powerful, and silent complicity in face of situations where human lives have been destroyed. I have also seen and shared in the process of involvement of many Christians and churches in the struggle for justice and human dignity. I have witnessed the renewal and enrichment of our churches in this process. But I have also observed that many groups and churches of the developed world still practise international aid in our continent by reinforcing and creating mechanisms of dependence and oppression. These practices confront the ecumenical movement with the great responsibility of continually pondering, on the basis of theological study, the church's mission in our continent so that aid may increasingly be an expression of solidarity and mutual understanding between these two worlds.

I have seen how attacks against Christians devoted to the poor have intensified, and for that very reason know how attempts have been made – on some occasions – to detract from and falsify the reputation of the WCC in the region. Nevertheless I have also seen how the witness of the WCC through the churches of the region has won the respect both of the people's organizations, of men and women of goodwill and of many sister churches.

During these years I have also been able to see how CICARWS has been evolving in understanding of its work, how it has increasingly included the struggle for justice and the need to eradicate the causes that produce the problems of inequality and injustice.

I did not want to close these pages without conveying what my experience in CICARWS has meant to me personally; I simply wanted to indicate what I think I have learnt, and what during these years, undoubtedly, I have *seen* and *heard*.

Our Ecumenical Diakonia – Both Large and Small

Alexandros Papaderos

Dr Alexandros Papaderos in this article contributes perhaps the most deeply theological part of this symposium. Written from the standpoint of the Orthodox churches it nevertheless illuminates profound issues for all churches sharing in the ecumenical movement. And here is a theologian who writes also of eggs, tomatoes and cucumbers!

★ ★ ★

The Orthodox Church has received invaluable material aid from the ecumenical community over the past forty years, chiefly through CICARWS (a very modest but convincing report on the World Council's activities in this field has recently been given by a faithful and long-serving member of its staff[1]). What I would like to stress from the outset is that to see only the material aspect of the aid we have received and to measure its value only in material terms would be totally to underestimate the real and effective value of this support and to misunderstand its true nature. One thing I shall try to do in this article, therefore, is to highlight some of the non-material, or at least not primarily material, aspects of ecumenical aid.

This is obviously no easy task – not just because, to the best of my knowledge, the Orthodox literature available on the subject has paid little attention to these aspects. The main difficulty is to disperse some of the fog still surrounding this matter and win through to some transparency on the other side. If I undertake this daunting task nonetheless, it is because I believe such an effort is long overdue.

One difficulty here, I must admit, is that we have been requested by the editor to tell something of our own involvement with people and events, and to do so through personal stories, adding

---

[1] Georges Tsetsis, *I Diekklisiastiki Synergasia stin Ellada*, Ekthesis Pepragmenon, 1983.

something about the significance these have had in our own lives. Visser 't Hooft has spoken of the dangers of writing an "I-book".[2] The dangers are no less, it seems to me, in writing an "I-article"! However, since we are all involved in the process of ecumenical learning and hope that one day our ecumenical fellowship will be transformed into an eucharistic fellowship, we must not only confess our sins and shortcomings to one another (James 5:16) but also confide our experiences, anxieties and hopes.

"Protestant eggs"

The day in October 1956 when I heard I had passed my final examination at the theological faculty of the University of Thessaloniki was a red-letter day. What better excuse for a party! Some of my fellow students and I were enjoying ourselves thoroughly when another student suddenly burst into the middle of the fun shouting " 'Buddha' wants you! Hurry!" "Buddha" was our nickname for our elderly professor of the history of religion who only a short time before had been congratulating me warmly on my final results. He had even awarded me a "distinction". We had nicknamed him "Buddha" not because of his interest in Buddhism but because, as far as the church's care for people and for the world was concerned, he had long since reached a state of Nirvana! Somewhat surprised, I now reported to his study where I found a nervous group of fellow students, general agitation and a stern-faced "Buddha" with nothing of Nirvana about him. Beside himself with rage he shouted at me: "You have failed my exam – and you will never pass it. Get out of my sight!"

What had happened? After two years it had belatedly come to the ears of our normally good-humoured professor that some of his theological students were working with Protestants, distributing clothing, food, medicine, etc., to various parishes in the town. In his view this could mean only one thing: surreptitious infiltration, proselytism – through his own theological students, no less. For him it seemed that the hour of the anti-Christ had come; he felt "the mystery of lawlessness already at work" (2 Thess. 2:6–7). When he questioned the other students about "collaborators" and discovered that I – his favourite student – had actually been the instigator of the outrage, his disappointment boiled over.

The background was this: a few years before some American Congregationalists had started an aid campaign in Thessaloniki. The city and the surrounding area, the birthplace of Alexander the Great, like the whole of Greece, was struggling in the miserable

---

[2] *Memoirs*, London, SCM Press, 1973, p. ix.

aftermath of the war and the civil war which had followed it. There were many orphaned children, homeless, unemployed refugees of all kinds and origins, old people who had lost their families, sick people, and people living in great fear and little hope. As the bishop of the city had entrusted me with the task of preaching in one of the worst-hit areas of the city, I was confronted almost daily with an anomalous situation: Tanoula, the Congregational-ists' Greek assistant, a charming and attractive Orthodox girl, with tremendous energy and commitment, was trying with little success to persuade the people to accept the strangers' gifts which they feared would harm their immortal souls. Our old bishop had had some ecumenical experience, even before the Amsterdam Assembly of the World Council which he attended as a participant, and also since then, so he was not long in accepting my suggestion (which had the full support of Tanoula and her employers) that it would be better to have groups of theological students carry out the distribution of the aid than to leave it to the foreigners. The people would then lose their fear and we students would have a chance to begin to understand the practical meaning of theology.[3]

With the bishop's blessing I set about organizing a "social work group" among the students and continued to lead it until I finished my studies. After that it was taken over and developed further by Prof. S. Agouridis and some other teachers. These groups later produced some outstanding priests and lay theologians, many of whom accompanied the thousands of Greek migrants abroad and are caring for them there.

Not a word of this valuable practical experience had reached the good professor of the history of religion until the day in question when I was examined and re-examined. After a somewhat stormy interview with me and a length telephone call to the bishop he informed me, not without visible signs of disapproval, that I had passed after all. Apparently the bishop had convinced him that our American friends could rightly claim that their effort "does not spring from error or uncleanness, nor is it made with guile" (1 Thess. 2:3).

At that time, too, the farm school run by the Quakers in Thessaloniki gave us eggs to distribute with the other goods. "Buddha" was the first but certainly not the last to suspect these "Protestant eggs" of proselytism and to paint the students' social commitment red, even though those eggs came from "capitalist" sources.

---

[3] "Wenn Theologie praktisch wird", in *Festschrift für Hauptpastor H. J. Quest, Hamburg*, ed. J. Sonnenberg, Stuttgart, Steinkopf Verlag, 1983. This contains some useful articles which are also relevant to diakonia.

Healing through diakonia

I have begun with this rather personal anecdote because it shows very clearly some of the points of friction that could be expected in inter-church aid in those days, and which have still not been entirely removed everywhere. These points of friction were deeply rooted in the Orthodox mind, solidly fixed by long historical experience. Since the Crusades and, still more so, since the Reformation, the meeting between East and West has almost always taken place on the ground of proselytism, not always conducted by the most elegant methods, and usually to the detriment of Eastern Christendom. Large areas of the East suffered for centuries under foreign domination, including "Christian" enthralment. Countless hundreds of Orthodox Christians suffered martyrdom for the sake of their faith, thousands lived a life of fear and terror as secret Christians. The gospel preached to them was not the good news of redemption, but dogmas and counter-dogmas. When the British and Foreign Bible Society announced its intention of preparing a translation of the Bible in modern Greek, the great scholar Adamantios Korais wrote:

> What fruit can a gift such as this bear among people who are groaning under the yoke of a cannibal and robber. Especially when the gift is offered by the Allies, the robber's friends and defenders. The British gift speaks of "isonomy" (i.e. equality), but their other behaviour has helped to keep us under the tyrant's yoke so that we continue to endure the suffering caused by its unlawfulness, and, worst of all, learn unlawfulness ourselves. No! No! Any gift they may give us, except freedom, is just a pretence and not a true act of benevolence.[4]

Nikiphoros Theotokis (1736–1800) who worked as a missionary among the Tartars accused Western proselytizers of impure intentions and meaningless efforts because they exploited the poverty of the people simply to win what later became known as "flour and rice Christians". He wrote:

> The lips of your proselyte have sworn but his soul has not believed. . . . What you have created therefore is not a Catholic, but a liar, a pharisee, a mocker of God. . . .[5]

With this historical background it will be clear that the real task for inter-church aid in our situation was not just to alleviate material suffering but, in doing that, to do something much deeper

---

[4] Alexandros Papaderos, *Metakenosis: Greichenlands kulturelle Herausforderung durch die Aufklärung in der Sicht des Korais und des Oikonomos*, Meisenheim am Glan, Verlag Anton Hain, 1970, p. 151.
[5] *Ibid.*, p. 148.

and more important, namely, to heal the wounds in the hearts of believers and in their historical consciousness. Deliberately or not, inter-church aid in Greece did in fact start such a process. The qualitative difference was at once apparent and people soon realized that this was not proselytism, but something radically new and different which was without precedent. Not even the early Christian *Logeia* corresponded to it, for the relationship between the Protestants of the West and the Orthodox of the East in the twentieth century was not the fraternal relationship that existed between the disciples in Antioch and Judaea (Acts 11:27–30) or between the Christians in Galatia and Corinth and the Christians in Jerusalem (1 Cor. 16:1–4) in the first century. In this case there was a long history of bad relations to redress, the barriers of many centuries to overcome. Money and materials to restore devastated churches, clothes for the naked, food for the hungry, medicines for the sick, homes for orphans, scholarships to help young theologians to study abroad, ecumenical work camps, development projects – all of these things were unquestionably valuable for their own sake. Yet the most important thing in all of them, everywhere, was this noticeable new quality of active, disinterested love.[6] Or at least not pursuing the old interest of proselytizing. For, although perhaps not explicitly and consciously tied in with it, the other result of this aid, the growing together into the ecumenical fellowship, was certainly present or at least expected as the fruit of growing trust.

The process of healing that I mentioned is by no means complete. Old wounds could begin to bleed again at any time, especially when zealots will not leave them alone. Other zealots on our Orthodox side still occasionally resort to reminders about "Protestant eggs" to disguise the lack of any substantial theological arguments against this growing ecumenical fellowship, or perhaps, if truth be told, against a social commitment which, though faithful to the gospel, is alien to custom and a habit of inertia. Despite this, however, the new quality in inter-church aid has become increasingly apparent, supported by other elements which I shall look at in greater detail below.

---

[6] According to John Chrysostomos (Migne, pp. 63, 83), we must show mercy to all human beings without distinction, whether they be monks or secular, Hellenes (heathens!) or Christians or even heretics, without considering whether they be worthy or not!

Creative challenge and response

Elsewhere I have expressed the opinion that "second only to the predominance of an atheistic system of government in many Orthodox countries, the ecumenical movement represents the major challenge to Orthodoxy in this century".[7] It is like a "gadfly" attached to the body of the church, stinging, irritating, troubling it as Socrates once did the conscience of the Athenians. This experience is no longer confined to the Orthodox but has now become a general experience of mutual challenge which extends to all Christians.

I am tempted briefly to consider this new situation in Christianity in terms of the contrasting yet harmonious ideas of challenge and response in order to see whether a certain parallel cannot perhaps be drawn between ecumenical development and cultural-morphological development.

These two notions are taken from the universal historical system proposed by A. J. Toynbee.[8] His analyses of the creative tension between challenge and response are, you remember, based on the approach of Chinese philosophy which sees the whole dynamic of all cosmic and historical events as a constant transition from Yin (a state of perfect creation, harmony, balance, peace) to Yang (incompleteness, instability, motion, activity) and back again to Yin. Alongside this "inward" factor in events Toynbee sets an "external" one, anything that acts as a stimulus to a culture from the outside at any given time, constituting a challenge, and forcing it into a testing situation (ordeal). When a culture is seriously challenged in this way the majority of people simply capitulate (a phenomenon of which the Westernization currently in progress throughout the world is a prime example). Few, if any, succeed in finding and giving a response to this challenge. To be really creative the response must do more than simply maintain or restore balance. It must be carried by an inner *élan vital* (Bergson), creating momentum, causing movement, for then and then only will a new challenge be provoked, eliciting a new response and so continuing life and moving it forward. Otherwise it is practically impossible for the culture in question to avoid stagnation or absorption into another culture.

Obviously we cannot simply transpose this kind of activist evolutionism, with its undertones of determinism, to the churches'

[7] "The 'Gadfly' on Trial: the 'Political' Commitment of the World Council of Churches", in *Voices of Unity, Essays in Honour of W. A. Visser 't Hooft*, Geneva, WCC, 1981, p. 79.
[8] *The Study of History*, 10 vols, London, 1934–1954, esp. Vol. I. Cf. also O. Anderle, *Das Universalhistorische System A. J. Toynbees*, Vienna, 1955.

relations with one another and try to understand the ecumenical development of this century in these categories. I use the terms "challenge" and "response" nonetheless, principally because many Christians today do in fact perceive these relations as just such a critical challenge and are firmly convinced that the response to it is proving more and more creative. Moreover, certain relatively meaningful analogies can certainly be drawn, even if only at the level of language. There is no denying, for example, that like the "arrested civilizations" the churches remained immobile for centuries. Over-adaptation to the geographical, cultural and historical conditions in which they existed had led them, as it were, to idolize their thinking, their action, the whole of their life, an idolatry of the outer crust of their heritage. Some of them had forgotten the specificity of the Christian way of life, the tightrope walking, the perpetual Exodus, and had become sedentary. Like certain nomads, they had settled in the oases of their present state. Toynbee speaks of *koros* (surfeit, satiety, spoiling by success, disgust), *hybris* (overweening arrogance, outrageous behaviour) and *ate* (disaster, blind impulse) as the causes of the breakdown of cultures which "rest on their oars".[9]

On the other hand, the factor which brought movement into the churches' relations with one another this century was unfortunately not an "inward" one but an "external" one. The first stimulus came not from an awareness of the sinfulness of our divisions, nor from repentance, love, truth or the will for renewal but primarily from the challenge of the external situation: the radical questioning of the Christian message, the destitution that followed the First and, still more, the Second World War, the persecution of Christians in many places, the groaning of the creation under new threats, the brokenness of our societies, the fear and despair of our peoples.[10] Before long, however, this external challenge stimulated an inner response in the form of the ecumenical movement. Phenomenologically and qualitatively speaking this was something quite new in church history, which

---

[9] *A Study of History*, Vol. IV, p. 258.

[10] The ecclesiological-pneumatological nature of the arguments on this subject in the letters of the Ecumenical Patriarchate which became so important for the ecumenical movement is all the more typical. "Patriarchal and Synodical Encyclical" of 1902; "Encyclical of the Ecumenical Patriarchate, 1920. Cf. *The Orthodox Church in the Ecumenical Movement*, ed. C. Patelos, Geneva, WCC, 1978, pp. 27–43. Nevertheless, even in these letters the concern for people and for humanity is clearly shown. The latter Encyclical actually mentioned acute needs and dangers and notes that "manifold dangers threaten not only particular churches, but all of them. These dangers attack the very foundations of the Christian faith and the essence of Christian life and society."

has known many outside stimuli and challenges but not so many inner responses!

It was in inter-church aid that this response made itself felt most tangibly and visibly, with the most immediate and creative effects. As long ago as 1920, the Encyclical of the Ecumenical Patriarchate, "Unto the Churches of Christ Everywhere", included among its eleven concrete suggestions for closer relations and cooperation among Christians everywhere: "whole-hearted mutual assistance for the churches in their endeavours for religious advancement, charity and so on", because "friendship and a kindly disposition towards each other can also be shown and demonstrated by willingness to offer mutual aid and help" and because "many good things will thus be achieved for the glory and benefit both of themselves and the Christian body". The Encyclical does not of course consider this mutual assistance as necessary "for its own sake", but as part of a comprehensive relationship and a new growing together into the love of Christ: "Above all, love should be rekindled and strengthened among the churches, so that they should no more consider one another as strangers and foreigners, but as relatives and as being a part of the household of Christ and 'fellow heirs, members of the same body and partakers of the promise of God in Christ' (Eph. 3:6)."[11]

In the early stages of the ecumenical era the position of Orthodoxy can be described, it seems to me, as both defensive and receptive. It was defensive, as ever, in its traditional refusal of Western proselytism, yet at the same time it was also receptive to the very things it rejected under the heading of proselytism.

---

[11] *Ibid.*, pp. 41–42. The ecumenical relevance of inter-church aid mentioned here was fully confirmed in the following centuries. The Orthodox consultation in Kiev (cf. *Just Development for Fullness of Life*, Geneva, WCC/CCPD, 1982, p. 19) notes: "Microdiakonia can also contribute to the healthy development of ecumenism. Our world is a divided world, and division is real not only among nations, but among Christians as well. Words alone are no longer adequate means to achieve unity, but deeds are needed to foster visible and concrete progress along the path towards unity. When Christians from different churches work together to serve fellow human beings in need, their love and concern for justice may serve to draw them together. Microdiakonia in ecumenical form can become an effective element in healing the divisions among Christians."

In his introduction to the Festschrift *Voices of Unity* (p. viii), Philip Potter says of my contribution: "The first generation of ecumenical leaders thought that doctrine divided but that service would unite. They had a point, as Alexandros Papaderos demonstrates with regard to the Orthodox churches. It was through the expression of love in service that these churches came into loving contact with the churches of the Reformation." The opposite is also true, as I have observed elsewhere (cf. *Oikoumenismos: Klisi kai proklisi*, Gonia, Chania, 1984, p. 39, note 1) and shall endeavour to show here.

Theology, music, icon painting, church order and church life in general all continued to show signs of Western influence long after the end of the nineteenth century. This receptivity of the Orthodox churches, which is entirely understandable from the historical point of view, had placed them in the position of being receivers, and this position was naturally reinforced and even intensified by inter-church aid. One of the psychological reasons underlying their hesitation is perhaps this: aid was accepted under pressure of need, to relieve the suffering of the people. In reality, however, the outward acceptance of material aid was accompanied by an inner attitude of defensiveness. The Orthodox response to this external challenge was, therefore, only in a limited sense creative, even though the aid was no longer given as a means of proselytizing but came as a challenge of love.

Not until some time later – it is difficult to pinpoint the moment exactly – did the Orthodox response to the ecumenical challenge begin to be truly creative both for Orthodoxy itself and for the whole fellowship of the churches. The ecumenical initiatives of the Patriarchate of Constantinople at the beginning of the century, which I have already mentioned, contained the seeds of many creative developments. Then came the great Orthodox diaspora which gave the West an open window on the Orthodox spiritual world, enabling Western Christians to see inside it and discover hitherto unsuspected spiritual treasures. Gradually the relationship became less "from-to" and much more "with" one another. The Orthodox response began to be less defensive. Apart from the great "offensive of love" under Patriarch Athanagoras, this response was generally cooperative rather than offensive; not dialectical in the sense of the interplay of Yin and Yang, mentioned above, but dialogical in the strength of the *Logos*, who took flesh and revealed himself as love, and as the way, the truth and the life. Inter-church aid thus ceased to be understood and carried out in a subject-object relationship in the tension of contact between East and West and became a substantive element in an entirely new reality of dynamic catholicity in which the Holy Spirit is the real stimulus of events, so that the formerly one-sided relationship could be transformed into genuinely creative interaction. Even microdiakonia (I define these terms below) which intervenes at specific, concrete points, is thus seen to be part of an all-embracing macrodiakonia in the ecumenical context.

Mutual enrichment

The speed and intensity with which this interaction progressed and developed can be seen from the example of the language. By this I do not mean the vocabulary only, but also and above all the spirit and ethos, the content of the language. Here Orthodoxy can claim with some justification to have given an effective and creative response to the ecumenical challenge, and to have offered its own gifts in return for the many spiritual and material gifts it has received. Although originally Greek, these gifts have long since become the property of the whole of Orthodoxy and should be seen as such. One need think no further than the many concepts, with their corresponding theological content, without which we would never have reached agreement today, and which are becoming all the more relevant the closer we move to a common expression of the apostolic faith. First of all there is the word *oikoumene* itself (and *oikos* with all its "living stones" as Philip Potter reminded us so vividly at the Vancouver Assembly of the WCC); and then the many others like *ekklesia-ekklesiologia*, *eucharistia*, *koinonia (sobornost)*, *martyria*, *liturgia* (and liturgy after the liturgy), *dialogue*, etc. as well, of course, as the term *diakonia* itself which concerns us particularly here.

Again, I would emphasize, the important thing is not so much the words as their content, the fresh insights, new perspectives, new approaches they convey, and in this we again have not one-sided giving and taking, but reciprocity, common reflection, mutual enrichment through sharing and participation. As far as the Orthodox world is concerned, this extremely creative process has received effective encouragement in recent years from the work of the Commission on Faith and Order, as well as from CICARWS and CCPD and the Orthodox consultations organized by them.[12]

I should like now to look at two concepts which are characteristic of the growing creativity in this form of work. These are "microdiakonia" and "macrodiakonia" which I shall try to define rather more clearly than has hitherto been done, demonstrating their content with some concrete examples.

I first proposed the two concepts of microdiakonia and macrodiakonia in my keynote address on "Liturgical Diakonia" at the "Consultation on Church and Service" organized by CICARWS and the Orthodox Task Force at the Orthodox Academy of Crete in November 1978.[13] In that address I emphasized that Christian diakonia is at one and the same time micro- and macro-dimensional

---

[12] *Orthodox Thought*, reports of Orthodox consultations organized by the World Council of Churches, 1975–1982, ed. Georges Tsetsis, Geneva, WCC, 1983.

[13] *An Orthodox Approach to Diaconia*, WCC, Geneva, 1980, pp. 17–46. Cf. Alexandros Papaderos, Diakonie II, Orth. Sicht, in *Ökumene-Lexicon*, Frankfurt/M, 1983, pp. 245–247.

and that the two must be carried out together as therapeutic and prophylactic philanthropy. By microdiakonia I mean "all the concrete measures taken by the Church to remedy the concrete distress of individuals by concrete means". (These include all the charitable institutions and organizations, and all the particular, individual demonstrations of love of the neighbour.) Macro-diakonia, on the other hand, means here all the measures which aim in the long term to make microdiakonia unnecessary! While recognizing all the inherent dangers of utopianism, I nevertheless believe that the Church today, though not neglecting micro-diakonia, should give absolute priority to macrodiakonia, both in its theological work and in its social commitment. Not with a view to building paradise on earth, but to prevent situations from being perpetuated on earth that look like images of hell. Macro-diakonia thus means conscious commitment to bringing about the kind of changes that will guarantee peace, promote justice, bring liberation, effectively fight against want and suffering, safeguard the dignity and rights of the human person and preserve the integrity of creation.

The Crete consultation, although it did not use the two terms itself, nevertheless fully accepted their content. This marked a new beginning with deep and lasting implications, as anyone familiar with the development of Orthodox theology and practice concerning diakonia in recent centuries will appreciate. Within a short time after its publication, the report of the consultation had set in motion a remarkable process of reflection, which was further encouraged in the ensuing years, amongst other things, by the inter-Orthodox meetings organized by the World Council of Churches. This is particularly true of the consultation on "Just Development for Fullness of Life: an Orthodox Approach" held in Kiev in 1982, when the concepts of micro- and macro-diakonia formed the main focus of the papers and discussions and gave rise to a new concept: *macrojustitia!*[14] Here, too, the stress is laid on the intrinsic oneness of diaconal service:

> (In reality, there exists only one diakonia . . . under two different forms: *microdiakonia* by and to individual members, and *macrodiakonia* as service to societies and their structures) and on their one common basis, which is agape, for love of God and humanity. Both diakonias

---

[14] The three subject areas of the consultation were: Orthodox theology of development; macrodiakonia of the Church on a general level; and micro- and macro-diakonia on personal, family, parish, social, state and international levels. Cf. *A Responsible Christian Participation*, Geneva, WCC, 1983.

are extensions of the eucharistic service. Both are a liturgy after the liturgy. Both express the missionary task of the Church.[15]

To anyone whose mental picture of Orthodoxy corresponds to A. von Harnack's description of it at the beginning of the century as "an ossified religious community", or to Oswald Spengler's view of Dostoievsky's authentically Orthodox thinking as the ultimate devaluation of the social by the metaphysical (as opposed to the supposedly Western-influenced thinking of Tolstoy which had produced the ultimate devaluation of the metaphysical by the social), the report of the Kiev consultation will come as a surprise. Sentences like these reveal the new awareness of macrodiakonia:

> In some cases, the Church's influence can extend to all aspects of society: social, economic, cultural and political life. The churches have a special God-given duty to work for the realization of justice and peace for the development of peoples and nations. The churches should be ready to defend human rights (freedom of conscience, freedom of speech, freedom of belief) and condemn their violations.[16]

If one reads some of the other documents of this consultation, for example, the brilliant contributions by Stanley Harakas, Metropolitan Geevarghese Mar Osthathios, Dimitrios Tsaoussis and others, it is soon apparent that such "revolutionary" sentences are by no means new and strange in Orthodoxy, but are firmly and legitimately founded in holy scripture and the tradition of the great Fathers of the Church, as the Crete consultation also demonstrated. What is new here is not the macrodiakonia mandate of the Church in itself, but our rediscovery and awareness of it. And for this we Orthodox can also largely thank the ecumenical fellowship. I say "also" because, like others, we did not simply take over a "foreign" theological property, for which we could again have had "Protestant eggs" thrown at us. Rather, it is the fruit of the Holy Spirit in our common effort of rethinking in the ecumenical fellowship, as Georges Tsetsis showed convincingly at the same Kiev consultation when he spoke of the "mutually enriching experience" achieved by the participation of the Orthodox churches in the World Council.[17] Julio de Santa Ana's contribution at the same consultation shows just how "mutual" this experience actually is.[18] Even an Orthodox theologian can largely subscribe to his ideas – and not just because of his eminently Orthodox vocabulary! This

---

[15] *Ibid.*, p. 17.
[16] *Ibid.*, pp. 17–18.
[17] "The Orthodox in the World Council of Churches", *ibid.*, pp. 41–47.
[18] "The WCC Sixth Assembly and Orthodox Participation", pp. 29–39.

whole process has increasingly shown itself to be a generally creative response to the ecumenical challenge to everyone, by everyone and everything.

The hard way forward

Despite these very positive developments we are, of course, still a long way from the final goal. A great deal of mature reflection is still required in our efforts for macrodiakonia to make sure that we do not confuse the vision of the kingdom with the vision of a comfortable existence, nor the fulfilled life we seek with what is simply a full life. Yet at the same time, with God's help, we need to do all in our power to bring movement where there is still immobility and apathy, wherever we are still blindly "resting on our oars". Let me give a few examples by way of illustration.

A few years ago, a far-sighted person recommended to us that the Orthodox Academy of Crete should encourage the people in one area of our island to start cultivating a piece of land which had lain untouched since the creation of the world. Helped by a team of Mennonites from Europe and America, we had already successfully promoted the use of greenhouses, a new economic development in our region, at our Centre for Agricultural Development as part of the wider macrodiaconal programme of the diocese of Kissamos and Selinon. The land that was to be brought under cultivation seemed ideally suited to growing cucumbers and tomatoes under glass. Over the years, however, poverty had left the area practically depopulated. For the people there, the one means of survival was to leave the land and emigrate. Not without some hesitation, we invited the farmers still living in the area to an initial information seminar for which we had deliberately chosen the title "Hope in the desert".

A second seminar followed, then a third and so on until the project could claim to be a great success. Finally we encouraged the farmers to form a cooperative and to be willing to include those of their compatriots who wanted to return from abroad, now that jobs and an opportunity to earn money had been created for them. Thousands of tonnes of tomatoes, cucumbers, etc., produced in this area are now on the market in Greece and Western Europe.

One of our priests, however, had great difficulty in fitting all this into his understanding of the mission and ministry of the Church. After the first seminar therefore he circulated a memorandum. It was the time of the military dictatorship in Greece, when any collective effort was regarded with suspicion as a possible plot. Talk of poverty and need did not suit the propaganda about rapid economic growth. Anyone who talked like that could only be a communist or a crypto-communist and was dealt with accordingly. If, into the bargain, one was dubbed a heretic by the Church one felt the rope tighten around one's neck. And heresy was precisely what the good priest thought we were engaged in. His argument was this: Christ came into the world to sow the seed of God's Word (Matt. 13) and not . . . tomatoes and cucumbers. How could an academy call itself Orthodox when it was busy caring for tomatoes and cucumbers?

The priest in question was basically a good-natured and very honourable Levite who had no intention of denouncing us and having us "put away". He was concerned only for the right continuation of the Church – the Church as *he* saw it, of course. As far as we could tell, the main difficulty was that he could see no connection between the foodstuffs in question and the liturgical-diaconal context, although for over fifty years he had been repeating in the Holy Liturgy the prayer: "For temperate weather, abundance of fruits of the earth, and for peaceful seasons, let us pray to the Lord." This difficulty, namely, thinking and acting in specific contexts, reveals a discrepancy which is a problem for many of us – the discrepancy between our theology and our prayers on the one hand, and our contact with the realities of the world and the needs of individuals and humanity on the other. A discrepancy of this sort is positively dangerous when set against the background of certain fundamental concepts of Orthodox theology and piety such as *pleroma* – fullness of life in the Holy Spirit, eucharistic understanding of the whole world, adoption and sanctification of matter with the removal of the polarity between the spiritual and the material, etc. In the report of the Crete consultation we read:

> Christian diaconia flows from the divine liturgy. . . . Each local celebration of the Eucharist is complete and universal, involving the whole of creation and is offered for the material and spiritual needs of the whole world.[19]

And that includes the need for tomatoes and cucumbers, for the possibility of returning home from abroad, for work, for hope.

Let me describe another example. Many people in our country, particularly priests and monks, are fond of evoking the Orthodox clergy's glorious tradition of commitment to the struggle for human dignity and liberation during the centuries of foreign rule suffered by a number of Orthodox nations. Not infrequently this

---

[19] *An Orthodox Approach to Diaconia, op. cit.*, p. 11.

struggle called for resolute and violent action. Although the clergy did not do this without considerable inner distress, they did it – and who would dare to criticize them for their action today? Indeed, on the contrary, even self-confessed critics and opponents of the Church praise them for this diakonia of liberation for which they had no need of a fully fledged theology of liberation. For them it was sufficient to know that the gospel is good news to the oppressed in that it brings salvation not only from sin, but also from the sinners, the tyrants who oppress them![20]

The same question exists today, but the answer is not so self-evident: what are the structures, the systems, the powers which today exploit, alienate, intimidate groups of people or even whole peoples, directly or indirectly enslaving them with modern methods and means?

At the beginning of the seventies we arranged a number of seminars for priests and others in positions of responsibility in our Church, when we dealt in depth with such issues. At the theoretical level we reached a broad measure of agreement, but it was a different story when it came to putting the theory into practice. For our practical work we chose to concentrate on the marketing system for citrus fruit. About six thousand families in our area of western Crete live mainly from growing the famous oranges of the region. *Live?* What does the word really mean here? Who actually *lives* off the hard work of these people? We knew that as well as the farmers themselves: the market was controlled by wholesalers and middlemen who captured the bulk of the profits for themselves. When we began to discuss a cooperative marketing system with the farmers and organized a public vote in a number of villages to decide on the matter, the dictatorship and the wholesalers were unanimous in condemning our action as un-Christian. When some priests even began to have doubts about whether this kind of involvement was really our affair, we and they together had to face the question of what really concerns us in this world. What makes us concerned? What must concern us?

I remember how much time we spent thinking about Christ's descent into hell at that time. He who holds the key of death and of hell (Rev. 1:18), before he rose again, descended into Hades, in other words, into the very centre of death. Even there, in the kingdom of the dead, of those who have cut themselves off from *koinonia* with God, that is, the powerful and the wealthy who have surrounded themselves unjustly with riches, the insatiable, those

---

[20] Alexandros Papaderos, "Skizzen aus dem Leben kretischer Priester", in "Wenn Theologie praktisch wird", *op. cit.*, pp. 230-245.

who have been led astray and those who lead others astray,[21] the Lord brought the Good News of the Gospel.[22] He descended "with great power" into Hades[23] and brought freedom, justice and peace.[24] Where else, until the *parousia*, can the real place of Christ's Church be, therefore, except wherever death prevails in relations between people. And what are the structures and mentalities which create injustice, exploitation, and coalition with Mammon, if not centres of death? Discipleship has always meant, and will always mean, being present with Christ in the centres of death, in solidarity with all those who have never lost sight of the vision of his kingdom, despite all their trials and tribulations, but also with those who have yet to gain, or regain, that vision. As we try to carry out our work of solidarity in the widest sense of macro-diakonia and plan our aims accordingly, we must together learn more about where the mission with which we are charged is calling us:

> If the Church is the church of Jesus Christ, it knows only one destination: the Kingdom of God. And all human goals must be critically analysed in the light of the information which we have received about the nature of that Kingdom and the road that leads towards it. The Church must therefore ask: which development, which emancipation, which revolution is in line with God's design?[25]

---

[21] Basil the Great, Comment. in Jes.1.497E (Migne, para. 30.322D and 498A, B (para. 30.393A).

[22] Clem., Str. 6.6 (para. 9, 268C).

[23] Acta Thomae A 156.

[24] Jn. Damasc, *De fide orth*, 3.29 (para. 94.1101A).

[25] W. A. Visser 't Hooft, *Memoirs, op. cit.*, p. 367. Emilio Castro is certainly correct in writing: "The teaching of Orthodox theologians on the transformation of the whole reality on the model of the transfiguration can help us in our understanding of the relation between history and eschatology." Equally correctly, for the Orthodox and everyone else, he adds: "This transformation is not an automatic process; it is a continuous search. It is an exposure of ourselves in worship to the action of God" *Sent Free*, Geneva, WCC, 1985, p. 80.

Ministering
to the Uprooted

Kathleen Ptolemy

Service to refugees has been an important function of Inter-Church Aid since its inception. In this article Mrs Kathleen Ptolemy tells of the continuing challenge of this work to the churches in years to come.

★ ★ ★

Anniversaries – a time for looking back to celebrate and evaluate, a time to look ahead, with a clearer vision and a clearer commitment to a strong and continuing partnership in the service to refugees.

My personal looking back does not stretch very far – only to 1980 – and yet for me those few short years in our CICARWS history have been filled to overflowing with experiences that have created a profound realization of a vital, caring, articulate and influential refugee network. The occasion of this anniversary allows me the pleasure of acknowledging and celebrating those people who have committed so much of their time and talents to promote just and generous responses to the refugees in our midst. Many names come to mind, too many to even begin to mention them – I salute them all, including all those unknown to me who have become part of a global refugee solidarity movement that has accomplished much but needs to meet even greater challenges in the future.

However, in our celebration of the past, the weight of the challenges of the present and future rests uneasily on our shoulders. Accomplishments of the past dim in comparison with the realities of the present and the needs of the future. Dramatic changes have taken place over the past decade that pose a whole new set of challenges to the churches and the CICARWS Refugee Service. No area of the world is now free of the political and social upheavals that will continue to give rise to refugee flows. Natural disasters are resulting in expanding numbers of homeless people. Restrictive migration laws are adding thousands of expellees to the roll call of the world's homeless. Visa restrictions and airline surveillance measures are dramatically increasing the populations of people who can no longer flee their country to seek protection elsewhere. These internally displaced people – refugees in their own midst – have little or no protection under international refugee conventions. As national domestic social service programmes are slashed in the face of economic recession and massive defence budget "priorities", refugees face greater and greater obstacles to their successful adaptation to their country of resettlement. In North America, Europe and South East Asia the "not welcome" signs are in prominent view for asylum seekers. Detention centres, movement and employment restrictions, incited racism and xenophobia, government propagated myths about economic refugees and job snatchers, and interdictions on the seas and in airports prevail. The world, it seems, has grown tired of refugees but is still energetically pursuing the very policies and practices that will inevitably give rise to new refugee movements.

What will the next forty years hold for the churches? Our experiences of the past show us that collective efforts will become even more crucial in view of increasing private governmental collaboration and the eroding power of the United Nations High Commissioner for Refugees (UNHCR) and other governmental agencies that appear to be more and more controlled by powerful member countries. The advocacy voice and the power of the church will need to be strengthened and not completely siphoned off by "hectic good works" that consume all our time, energy and skills. The vast networking system that the churches have built up, rather shakily over the past, needs to be acknowledged and systematically strengthened. The Christian imperative to seek justice will need to be exercised in ways that are competitive with countervailing forces. And the enormous power for change that is rooted in the base communities, the grassroots, will need to be promoted and enabled to flourish to create just and sustainable changes.

Local churches in the CICARWS network and local churches in all parts of the world through their refugee experiences have undergone dramatic changes in their ministry to refugees in their midst and in their commitment to the principle of justice as mission abroad. This swelling of localized involvement in refugee concerns is a far cry from the not too distant past when, for most parishes and congregations, refugees were "somewhere over there", a cause for earnest, prayerful concern on appropriate occasions and for financial contributions to specific appeals. That has changed. There is scarcely a congregation anywhere in the world today whose collective life has not been affected by the refugee situation in one way or another. Local churches have become critical to the safety and wellbeing of the journey of countless numbers of refugees from flight to permanent protection.

Countries of origin

Escape

"How did you manage to escape?" "I was helped by the church." How many times has that story been told and retold by those refugees who have made the most dramatic decision of their lives: to leave home, community and homeland, to depart from friends and often family rather than bear the threat of persecution for reasons of their race, religion, nationality, membership in a particular social group or political opinion. Once they have crossed the border into a foreign country they may fall under the protection of international conventions and protocols designed to assure their protection but until that border is crossed they are dependent upon their own resources and, often, the assistance of local churches. The task of ensuring the safety of someone fleeing the threat of persecution is always risky, often clandestine in nature. For many fleers the options are not legal but quiet departures, entries, often illegal, into neighbouring countries. The available options open the fleer to a variety of vulnerabilities: tip-offs to the authorities, exploitation by "cayotes" and dealers in forged documentation, bribery and theft. Local churches have often played a life-saving role in assisting in the escape of refugees and the importance of this work will increase as the barriers to border crossing increase and threaten the most fundamental right of refugees – to flee.

Human rights advocacy

Churches in refugee-producing countries have also been called to an increasingly important role in providing the type of documentation necessary to ensure effective advocacy at national and international levels. Documentation of disappearances, extrajudicial killings, torture, unprovoked military attacks, the collection of testimonies of the victims of gross human rights violations; local churches are being called on to provide witnesses and testimonies, acts that threaten their very existence. Examples are countless. The testimonies of local church people all through Central America and in many parts of Africa have brought to international attention incidents of atrocities that otherwise would have been hidden from world attention.

Internally displaced persons

Local church workers are also on the front line in terms of providing assistance to internally displaced people who cannot flee their country. It is often the local parish that becomes the safe haven for internally displaced people who cannot leave their countries. These are the high risk tasks that the church is being called upon increasingly to perform, and the costs are high. Legal battles and even death have befallen church workers within the last decade who have stood on the side of the victims of persecution. The strain on the local church is intense: who, for instance, is a victim of persecution in need of assistance to escape; who is a fugitive; when should the church take actions that are contrary to the laws of the land? The issues are hard and divisive but the decision to risk in favour of the refugee has often been empowering. Issues and the biblical mandate have converged for many to provide a clear sense of purpose. The story of the Exodus has had profound meaning for those local churches faced with these life-risking challenges as it becomes clear that it was part of God's plan to uproot people out of their slavery and oppression and to secure their futures where they could once again glorify God.

Countries of first asylum

Decisions

Fleeing one's country is just the beginning of the refugee's search for protection. New and increasingly formidable threats to the refugee's need for protection exist in the majority of today's countries of first asylum. When refugee flows first begin, it often falls to the local church in the area of reception to provide hospitality, safety and material assistance, and to alert the international community to the need for additional assistance. Small, often impoverished, churches in border areas around the world have lived out their conviction that Christians are called to love their neighbour and to "prove neighbour" to the suffering world. This call to hospitality to the stranger is being sorely tested. The results of the Christian conviction that "you are my neighbour" have led to legal charges of aiding and abetting aliens and to disrupting community relationships where existing resources and group tensions are already tightly stretched. For many of these churches facing the challenges presented by the unexpected arrivals of refugees in their midst the past few years have challenged, rocked and usually renewed.

In Europe and North America the phenomenon of large numbers of non-European refugees arriving as asylum seekers is relatively recent, and is obliging local parishes to become familiar with the complexities of immigration laws and asylum procedures. Local church groups must now become para-legal experts, advocates, and often the sole supporters of those asylum seekers who are unable to avail themselves of the social, medical and legal benefits available to recognized residents. Churches are increasingly faced with the need to determine their responsibilities to refugees whom their governments will not recognize as such. These wrenching challenges, once the concern of a handful of experts, are now the everyday concerns of thousands of parishes situated in areas receiving asylum seekers.

Extending protection

The question of legal protection, in the past the prerogative of the UNHCR, has become an increasingly important issue for the churches. More and more persons who have genuine protection needs are being prevented from claiming asylum or are rejected and deported. The issue of protection in Europe, North America, Australia and New Zealand was the subject of a CICARWS consultation in Canada in 1984 which brought together 35 persons representing churches and ecumenical agencies from 13 Western countries. Four crucial areas of asylum and protection were discussed: extending protection to victims of civil strife and others in refugee-like situations; ensuring protection to asylum seekers on arrival; assuring safe haven to refugees in our midst; building church relationships and advocacy.

The depth of the conversations and the intensity of the debate revealed the seriousness of the implications of the churches' role in providing protection to refugees where decisions based on justice and human rights concerns bring them into opposition with their own governments. After much debate the consultation affirmed "the churches' responsibility to provide for emergency protection and to advocate longer term processes which will move our governments towards equity and consistency in the determination of refugee status".[1] A deceptively simple statement, yet one that has brought the global Christian refugee network into full solidarity with the churches in the United States who have declared themselves sanctuary churches. In 1985, over 140 churches and synagogues were providing sanctuary to undocumented Salvadorean and Guatemalan refugees in the USA. The sanctuary move-

---

[1] *Protection of Asylum Seekers in Western Countries*, report and recommendations of the World Council of Churches consultation, Niagara Falls, Ontario, Canada, 15–18 May 1984, p. 29.

ment has highlighted one of the clearest examples of the churches' comprehensive ministry to refugees through an identification of a particular group's need for protection based on an interpretation of recognized refugee definitions and the development of analysis of the situation that has forced so many thousands to flee these countries and provided the common base for advocacy in areas of foreign policy, arms expenditures, human rights violations and refugee determination criteria. Material assistance has been given freely and the refugees protected through the sanctuary movement have, through their public witness, assumed a prophetic role that has given churches worldwide the opportunity to rediscover the gospel and the essence of the ministry to refugees.

Other protection concerns demanding the advocacy of the churches involve ensuring access by the refugee claimant to fair and equitable determination procedures. The issues are complex, requiring new initiatives by the churches to facilitate admission at ports of entry for asylum seekers and to monitor determination procedures in an attempt to combat measures being introduced that limit the refugee claimant's right to a fair hearing.

The signs of the times are stark, clear and full of challenge. Churches have gained, and will need to increase, expertise as watchdogs, legal experts, political analysts and advocates and committed information-sharers in order to promote the protection of refugees.

Assistance

In many first asylum countries the local church plays an increasingly significant role in providing protection, material assistance and pastoral care. The UNHCR "cares for ten million refugees", according to its latest publications. For those refugees local churches often play a vital role in providing additional assistance, pastoral care and advocacy, and thousands of lives have been saved by their efforts.

However, the majority of today's refugees, estimated to be about 25 million, are not assisted by the UNHCR. They are to be found displaced within their own country or hidden in the countrysides of neighbouring countries, eking out an existence as migrant workers, in the cities where they become part of the faceless mass of millions subject to poverty, exploitation and the constant fear of insecurity that comes from temporary or illegal residence status. They are to be found in virtually every corner of the globe; refugees in every sense of the word who are unable or unwilling to seek the protection afforded by a legal recognition of their status. How many of these refugees have been assisted by the local church? It is difficult to know but by any count the numbers must be significant. For many refugees the church is the only institutional link with their earlier lives that they feel able to trust in a first asylum situation where "officials spell danger".

Temporary protection

For many refugees their country of first refuge is a place of temporary exile where their presence may be tolerated but the prospects of long-term integration are bleak. The reasons for this disturbing trend are numerous. Most refugees arrive in countries that constitute the less materially developed world often vulnerable to political instability, maldevelopment and external influences. The call from these countries for international burden sharing is generally met with an inadequate response. Refugees bring to the surface racial and ethnic prejudices and are generally perceived as adding to existing unemployment and political instability problems. The refugees are forced to exist for years in conditions that create serious social problems arising from their inability to resume normal life patterns of family living and economic independence. It is in the addressing of these concerns that the churches have played perhaps the most dramatic but least heralded role in their ministry to refugees. Local churches, as part of the community, and not an externally imposed aid agency, have been faced with the need to search for creative ways to respond to their biblical understanding of the stranger or sojourner who has come to seek refuge in their community.

The task is not easy, especially in those situations where the refugee's stay is of a temporary nature either because the host government is unwilling to provide for local integration or because the refugee is seeking temporary refuge in anticipation of return home or third country resettlement. Churches in these situations have been faced with incredible challenges to maintain the self-esteem of the refugee awaiting an uncertain future. As resettlement and repatriation opportunities diminish the problems increase. Refugees rejected for resettlement linger on in growing despair for their future, social problems increase, and self-reliance programmes designed to help bridge the gap between flight and permanent resettlement become symbols of false hope.

Although the continent of Africa has maintained its commitment to local integration and voluntary repatriation for refugees, the implementation of these policies has been severely hampered by natural disasters, economic recession, continuing new waves of refugees and the failure of the international community to provide sufficient additional development funding to host countries. Local

Top: The churches assisted Hungarian refugees in Austria in 1956...

Left: ... and enabled returning refugees in South Sudan to rebuild a school, 1973

Above: CIMADE workers distribute foodstuffs to displaced families in France, during the Second World War

Photos: WCC, Margaret Murray

Right: The churches assisted Palestine refugees...

Below: ... and Tibetans in India, 1961

Photo (below): Walter Kilpatrick

churches, assisted through an internationally unique, ecumenically coordinated refugee service have developed programmes that provide personal support and assistance to thousands of refugees whose needs cannot be adequately met by international aid agencies. The leadership taken by African churches in defining and responding to the responsibilities of local churches has provided leadership for all churches who face similar situations in their own countries. The African churches have identified pastoral care as a priority.

> Pastoral care . . . is central to the life and ministry of the Church. To offer educational or financial assistance to refugees, to help them start self-help projects, or to build awareness of the situations which cause refugees, are all commendable activities which can be undertaken by any concerned individual or organization . . . the Church has more to offer, and must offer it.[2]

Counselling to enable refugees to recover, adjust and plan realistically for the future; awareness building in the community; special assistance to vulnerable refugees; contributing to refugee self-reliance through educational assistance, counselling and self-help projects; and the promotion of informal study and recreation programmes, these priorities for local church involvement have given practical guidelines, born out of the experiences of our church partners facing the largest global refugee crisis that will strengthen the global network's sense of purpose and mission.

Finding permanent solutions

The UNHCR, churches and governments define their goal of providing durable solutions through three options listed in order of priority: voluntary repatriation, local integration, and third country resettlement. These traditional solutions which in the past resolved the needs of many refugees now are applicable in only a limited number of cases. Millions of refugees live in despair of finding lasting solutions. Home for many is a detention centre, a humane deterrence centre, an airport lobby or a church basement.

Voluntary repatriation, going home, is the one sustaining dream of the refugee, no matter how many years he has lived in exile, and yet the options today to return are remote for all but a few. Where repatriation is possible local churches have played important roles both in counselling and assuring that the repatriation is indeed voluntary, and in providing assistance to the refugee upon his

---

[2] *Handbook for Refugee Workers*, Refugee Service, All Africa Conference of Churches, 1983, p. 88.

return. Through church networking, assessments are shared with the refugee regarding the situation he is likely to face upon his return; churches in the receiving country are often alerted in order to ensure a welcome and initial assistance. This informal networking is also being used increasingly to alert receiving churches to the return of deportees whose needs upon return will be significant.

Local integration

The practice of local integration in countries of first asylum is no longer simple or automatic. In the past local integration was relatively straightforward when refugees fled to neighbouring countries where local customs, language and employment opportunities were similar to those left behind. Local integration possibilities, except in Africa, now require enormous adaptation and integration efforts by the refugee. Faced increasingly with the need to seek their own permanent solutions refugees are seeking asylum in countries where customs, language and employment loom as barriers to successful integration. The involvement of the churches in facilitating local integration requires a complement of skills that pose new challenges. Language training, often not provided by governments for asylum seekers, has become a major programme priority of many churches. Refugees given refugee status by governments often fail to qualify for government-assisted resettlement programmes. The challenges faced by these people are formidable: information regarding access to social services systems is often lacking, counselling regarding language training opportunities, housing options, medical services is minimal. Churches have been challenged to play a vital role in these integration services, particularly for those groups of refugees who arrive in countries where there are no established ethnic groups able or willing to identify with the newly-arrived refugees. They now find themselves in the difficult situation of ministering to refugees across language barriers, social and religious differences with no help from non-existent ethnic support groups.

The challenge to the church to provide effective local integration will increase dramatically in light of refugee migration across regional borders.

Third country resettlement

Traditionally the world has looked to Europe, North America, Australia and New Zealand and to other countries of immigration to provide opportunities for permanent resettlement for refugees who are welcome, unsafe or for whom there are no local integration solutions in the country of first asylum. When at the invitation of CICARWS churches met together in May 1983 in Stony Point, USA, to discuss refugee resettlement it was clear that the UNHCR's third option was up against as many problems as the first and second.

> The era of refugee resettlement has now ended. The years of significant refugee and migration movements were years of rapid development and sustained economic expansion in the industrialized West. They were years of full employment. The OECD countries' economies (countries where most refugees have been resettled) are entering recession; the International Council on Social Welfare reports that "most industrialized nations are entering the 1980s in a state of economic uncertainty, the twin pillars of inflation and unemployment have increased to serious proportions, and the European Trade Union Confederation talks of 'catastrophic developments' and a 'disastrous' employment situation in Europe!"[3]

The consultation participants went on to note a number of developments related to this situation that directly affect refugees and migrants:
- restrictive border policies with a related increase in police and legislative action;
- blatant *refoulement*[4] policies by governments with little fear of reproach;
- the increasing anxiety on the part of host-receiving countries to "foreigners" in their midst has provided opportunities for a significant growth and development of racist organizations;
- increased opportunities for the manipulation and exploitation of refugees, in particular refugee and migrant women.

Within the context of these realities the participants recognized, two main challenges in the task of resettlement and integration:
- how to ensure adequate national resettlement policies and programmes at a time when general political and economic forces mean that governments are becoming increasingly hesitant about taking even more refugees;
- how to ensure that refugees are not integrated at the expense of other oppressed and exploited groups, or used to threaten their struggle for justice.[5]

The message from this resettlement consultation was prophetic. Individual church parishes who may once have seen their role in

---

[3] *Draft Consultation Highlights*. World Council of Churches Stony Point Consultation on Refugee Resettlement, Stony Point, New York, 1983, pp. 1–2.
[4] Rejection or return across the border.
[5] *Ibid*, p. 3.

the resettlement of refugees as a good works service to individuals have increasingly become involved in broader concerns that bring social justice concerns to their doorstep. Refugee-assisting parishes must make hard decisions about who they will help for many of the refugees in their midst have no status, no government recognition or support. As economic conditions deteriorate church groups face difficult decisions regarding the future of "their" refugee – better a sweatshop, dead-end job or longer-term assistance in assessing systems? Middle-class churches have had to discover the hidden side of their cities – welfare system, job exploitation, housing conditions of the poor, indifference of government officials. They have learned to rely on the services and support of ethnic organizations and have come to a clearer understanding of their unique role in providing ongoing personal support, comfort and encouragement rather than the maintenance and financial support which is more properly the responsibility of government. New models of partnership between government and churches are being worked out within the context of a clear church understanding of its appropriate role as a partner with unique strengths in areas of resettlement support where it is inappropriate or ineffectual for a government to act. It has become a priority concern of churches in resettlement countries everywhere to ensure that governments plan their annual refugee levels on the basis of an adequate response to global resettlement needs and not on a calculation of the resources of the private sector to "do the job".

Conclusion

"The earth is the Lord's and the fullness thereof, the world and they that dwell therein." James Cogswell in his book *No Place Left Called Home* uses a statement of the Second Vatican Council to express more fully this biblical theme that has such profound implications for our continuing journeying with the refugees.

> God intended the earth and all that it contains for the use of every human being and people. Thus as all people follow justice and unite in charity, created goods shall abound for them on a reasonable basis. . . The right to have a share of earthly goods sufficient for oneself and one's family belongs to everyone.[6]

Our earthly goods include not only food and shelter but structures that ensure justice, protection and dignity for all. The distribution of these goods, so essential to life, is determined by principles that for the Christian recognize the sovereignty of the Lord

---

[6] Friendship Press, New York, 1983, pp. 7–8.

and the call to promote a Christian understanding of stewardship. This we believe or not, we take action, or by not taking action support those powers that seek out of greed to oppress and to control what is not their's to control. For those thousands who have journeyed in the past with refugees glimpses have been caught of that reality and reinforced in this statement:

> It is the refugee who reveals to us the defective society in which we live. He is a kind of mirror through whose suffering we can see the injustices, the oppression and maltreatment of the powerless by the powerful.[7]

To act more forcefully and with a clear understanding of the complexity of the challenge and the necessary responses – there is much to be done but the base is secure and rooted firmly in the experiences, deeds, courage and faith of the refugees and the local churches throughout the world who continue their journey with the refugees.

> Refugees are left without power and protection, but they live by hope; hope in God's ultimate justice; hope that basic grace will open up new life (John 1:51). They rekindle in us the faith in our resurrection; beyond tribulation, beyond martyrdoms in repressive nation states there will be liberation; there will be bread for all; there will be a secure home; there will be peace; there will be wellbeing (shalom).

> This is our faith, rooted in the Bible and the history of God's people.

---

[7] Statement by refugee worker, Africa 1980, quoted in *Draft Consultation Highlights*, Stony Point, New York, 1983, p. 4.

Inter-Church Aid
and the Future

Jean E. Fischer

Mr Jean Fischer, who served CICARWS in several capacities, and finally as director in years of great change, reflects in this article on his experience and gives pointers to the direction in which this work of the ecumenical movement must go in the coming years.

★　★　★

After the 1961 New Delhi Assembly, DICARWS was given new responsibilities. Whereas up to then inter-church aid had been practised mainly in Europe, it was now becoming increasingly clear that WCC service activities must also be extended to other continents. The new mandate in short was "to express the ecumenical solidarity of the churches through mutual aid in order to strengthen them in their life and mission and especially in their service to the world around them (diakonia)".

In 1961 the "young" churches of Africa and Asia came on the scene in the WCC, as did (more fully than before) the Orthodox churches. The ecumenical stage was no longer limited to one region of the world. For the African continent, the wind of independence had just swept across colonies and churches. Many of them had become "independent" of the missionary societies, and were gathering their energies to take part in the vast exertions demanded of the new nations by the nation-building process. The wider membership of the WCC opened out for Inter-Church Aid, whose role had been to share in the work of church reconstruction after the Second World War, the prospect of extending mutual aid, Christian service in the widest sense, to the churches and inhabitants of the new countries. The challenge was "to help meet the needs on behalf of humanity and without any distinction of creed, race, caste, nationality or politics".

After spending seven years in Northern Rhodesia (now Zambia) as a missionary, I was appointed in 1964 to the staff of DICARWS. At that period, the WCC and DICARWS were establishing the

programmes and structures needed to carry out their activities as
defined by the 1961 New Delhi Assembly, and were interested in
particular in the African continent.

Dr Z. K. Matthews, my colleague in the Africa Desk, and I had
the task of investigating the new situation in independent Africa.
This situation was causing concern, and already numerous refugees, the needs of development and equipment in the domains of
education and health, pointed to a gigantic task awaiting the churches of Africa and the ecumenical community as a whole. We
accordingly conducted an extensive inquiry among the churches
of nearly all the African countries. Dr Matthews, Sir Hugh Foot
(later Lord Caradon), the Rev. James Lawson, associate general
secretary of the All Africa Conference of Churches, and I under-
took several lengthy visits to Africa.

Numerous extremely interesting talks with political and government personalities and with church leaders quickly convinced us
that the problems of independent Africa required from the churches
an imaginative, substantial and financially considerable contribution. It also became clear, however, that their contribution
would be meaningful only if national strategies and plans could be
established in collaboration among churches, Christian councils
and the authorities on national and regional level. Furthermore, it
became equally obvious that the international ecumenical
community would have to raise considerable funds to finance the
educational, medical, social and even agricultural programmes
which the African churches were proposing to promote. Consequently in 1965 the Ecumenical Programme for Emergency Action
in Africa (EPEAA) was launched in collaboration with the All Africa
Conference of Churches. At the time this was the biggest DICARWS
programme, and aimed to raise ten million dollars over a five-year
period. On similar lines, other programmes were also promoted,
such as the Christian Committee for Service in Algeria (CCSA)
dealing with reconstruction in Algeria after the devastation of the
war, together with various other considerable undertakings, in
Asia in particular. It was, I think, this experience of the investigation in Africa and the numerous contacts made with devoted,
enthusiastic persons determined to move mountains in the service
of the African peoples, which firmly implanted in me several
convictions which were the driving force of my actions during my
eighteen years of ministry in the Commission on Inter-Church
Aid and which the following pages are intended to explain.

At the 1968 Uppsala Assembly, the aspirations of peoples freed
from colonial rule or still struggling for liberation were a marked
feature of the debates. The 1966 Church and Society conference

had struck the keynote: "Justice, not charity". The third world was making itself heard, and the essential requirements of development and justice, sharing and solidarity, were already shaping various new WCC programmes. It was noticeable that the DICARWS report to the Assembly included a certain number of "open questions" which had arisen in inter-church aid circles, and which underlined the need for DICARWS to equip and adapt itself to the challenges of the world and the expectations of the churches of the third world continents.

The Uppsala Assembly thus presented DICARWS with a new task: that of bringing together the churches and getting them to pool their resources to meet the needs of the time; of giving concrete form to the vision of a fellowship of churches which would not be satisfied merely to cooperate after the fashion of states, but would seek to live the community of the universal church; of becoming a world diaconal fellowship in the service of humanity, in which "no one said that any of the things which he possessed was his own, but they had everything in common" (Acts 4:32).

We must remember that in 1968 in Uppsala and in the world generally, people had the impression that the gap between rich world and poor world could be filled by increasing the budgets for aid and cooperation by a small percentage. Unfortunately there has been a rude awakening since. Even in the churches themselves we are far from having achieved any such pooling, sharing of gifts, talents, means and resources available in each church. Immediately after the Uppsala Assembly, I was placed at the service of the All Africa Conference of Churches (AACC) to organize its second assembly. Based in Abidjan, I spent a year rich in contacts and relations with the African churches which made it possible for me to deepen my knowledge of the aspirations and aims of these partner churches of DICARWS. While on the one hand these churches wished to be treated as equal partners with the rest and refused to be treated as beggars for aid, they also wished to play their own part in the world ecumenical movement and were convinced they could make an authentic, positive and valid contribution, even if it were not one that could be measured in dollars.

On my return to Geneva at the end of 1969, I was given the task of coordinating operations on the project list and the regional secretariats of DICARWS. I set about this task with the questions which I had brought back from Africa, which seemed to me important for the integrity of the ecumenical movement: How can churches "poor in money" but "rich in life" be incorporated into the world fellowship of mutual aid which we were trying to establish? How can they be justly valued and brought to make their contributions to the various aspects of inter-church aid? How must we avoid regarding and treating them as mere recipients of the manna bestowed by the aid and service agencies of the churches?

Was it possible to create that fellowship of partners which would enable each and all to mobilize considerable energies and initiate programmes appropriate to a Christian witness of unity and justice?

My new duties gave me various opportunities to take part in regional meetings in Asia, the Near East and many other continents and countries. Everywhere the essential theme concerned the need to find a right style of relationship between donors and receivers of inter-church aid. Was it possible on the inter-church plane to develop different attitudes from those prevailing on the plane of states or intergovernmental organizations, where the rule was "he who pays the piper calls the tune"?

In 1971 I was convinced that the project system was out-of-date, that it no longer matched either the needs of the work of the churches of the developing countries, or the vision we had of a fellowship of action in which the talents and resources of each and all would be pooled in order to manifest the unity already achieved within an ecumenical movement.

In a memorandum to Alan Brash, director of DICARWS, I presented a diagnosis of the project system and of the WCC project list.

> The project system has now been operating for nearly twenty years
> . . . many projects have been formulated, financed and implemented
> . . . but in a dispersed order . . . independently from one another,
> often for prestige reasons or for denominational interests. Little overall
> planning has been done and one rightly ought to ask whether such
> projects have had a sizeable impact on national situations. . . The types
> of projects proposed by the churches have not always been responses
> to critical problems of the national communities. . . The DICARWS
> projects analysis shows that few projects have aimed at treating the
> root causes of underdevelopment such as agrarian reform, workers
> unions, farmers unions and cooperatives, housing, unemployment and
> other "justice" concerns.

I suggested a radical move: to pause and reflect on what the ecumenical fellowship of donors and receivers were doing together, and what they ought to correct in their common enterprise.

> – Declare a moratorium on projects for 1971 and 1972, ask donors to
> make resources available for funding a responsible planning and
> study process as well as an evaluation of the last ten years of project
> activity in each country.

– Initiate a series of regional "confrontation" meetings where donors and receivers or "beggars", as some call themselves, would reflect together on the meaning of fellowship. . . Are the resources of the church universal to be labelled Western, Eastern, etc . . . . or do they belong to all?

In his reply, the DICARWS director affirmed the need to take a serious look at the project system, bearing in mind the consequences that such an exercise could have on the division.

The project system is not as bad as you describe it. It is however sufficiently bad to justify a real re-examination . . . you have to give the Divisional Committee a real challenge but also a real alternative between adopting a document which would in fact improve the operation of the project system to our best wisdom at this moment, but also the chance to do something more radical, as you suggest in your memo.

From that time, the project system was subjected to analyses and discussions which quickly showed that to call that system in question disturbed a whole network of well-oiled and well-tried operations more or less matching the North-South relations of the period on the level of governments and intergovernmental institutions.

To lay hands on the project system was in fact to raise the question of the nature of the relations between "rich" and "poor" churches; it raised questions of ecclesiology. It meant questioning both sides on the quality of the ecumenical community, on attitudes in regard to money, to questions of power, denomination, interdependence, solidarity – in short it meant radically to call in question the existence, aims and functions of the Division of Inter-Church Aid.

In the following years 1971–1975, conversations went ahead briskly with the whole team of CICARWS regional secretaries and other representatives of inter-church aid and Christian service agencies or the churches. They were not always easy or sympathetic, with everyone defending their point of view stoutly and with conviction. But while all readily acknowledged the need for a better organization of the ecumenical community, I was always surprised at the force of inertia and resistance to change that emanated from our partners once the topic of sharing money was mentioned. A sort of cautious conservatism.

In 1971 I submitted a paper to the Commission entitled "Beyond Cooperation to Community":

How can the Commission, as part of Unit II – Justice and Service, and as part of the World Council of Churches and the ecumenical movement, improve its services and programmes, so as to change from an instrument of cooperation in many fields into an instrument through which the underlying unity of the churches will be manifested; change from an occasional gathering of peoples round a conference table into a living community? There is a growing concern for a deeper and more real *partnership* in the whole business of sharing resources. . .

I submit that one of the tasks of the Commission is to give content to such words as *partnership* and *dialogue*. . . If a real sense of partnership is to develop, it will involve a deeper mutual understanding between those responsible for the allocation of resources from the so-called donor countries and the leaders of the churches who request these resources for work in their own countries. Such understanding can only develop out of personal contacts and an actual sharing of experience. . .

Quite obviously, the WCC task of "assisting the churches to express their solidarity" can only be fulfilled if all parties concerned have a genuine commitment to ecumenical cooperation and sharing, and if they all demonstrate a willingness to conceive of both needs and resources as belonging to the whole church.

In 1971 the CICARWS Commission agreed to undertake a revision of the project system by stages, and to complete this task by the next WCC Assembly in 1975 in Nairobi.

The first steps in the reform involved two elements:

– giving greater autonomy and responsibility to the regions; in this way the regional groups were placed in a position to decide and follow the course of inter-church aid relations and of the way projects operated in each region (continent) in accordance with the particular features of the regional context;
– establishing a category of "priority" projects decided by the originators themselves with the proviso that the donors must respect the priorities determined by their partners, but also that the originators must make a real effort to analyze what the priorities should be.

Although this reform made it possible to decentralize the decision-making process and to redistribute power to some extent, it is obvious that it made no fundamental change in the system itself. A piecemeal project-by-project approach could not generate the impact needed even to spur the churches to act together in their own respective countries. The financing of numerous small projects could not influence the processes of development. On the contrary, people could see that the churches, the denominations, were competing with one another to attract as much of this manna as possible.

In 1973, half way through the reform after two years full of conversations, consultations and strenuous debates on various levels, I submitted to CICARWS a document entitled "Whither the Project System?" which caused something of a stir and had some difficulty in being accepted. Some people did not hesitate to call the document irresponsible, doctrinaire, and other pejorative names. Yet that paper was the result of team work and simply reflected the deep-seated aspirations of numerous colleagues in the international network of inter-church aid.

> When one talks of dialogue and respect between partners, what are the factors which must govern the relationships and lead to decisions about sharing? Can we in the future envisage a relationship whereby with mutual confidence between men with the same spirit of service and dedication, there can be a reciprocal sharing of troubles and joys, worries and resources, in a real climate of co-responsibility which will no longer place such importance on technical dossiers, complicated questionnaires, and slow and unwieldy procedures, but reach a better re-distribution of the resources which God has entrusted to his church scattered over the six continents?

The document dealt with the multiplicity and compartmentalization of aid, multilateral and bilateral, with the growing opposition to the project system and doubts about its ability to meet the needs of the time. It also raised the question of the identity and autonomy of partners within the ecumenical fellowship.

> If we have today arrived at a point where a malaise corrupts the relationships between members of the fraternal fellowship, it is indispensable that these relationships be radically transformed, however painful and costly this may be, as much for those who give as for those who are accustomed to receive.

Two main lines of research were suggested:

– The aim of aid is the "end of aid." Thus, all aid should be given in such a manner that those who receive it will become more autonomous, and less dependent. If the aid becomes an estrangement, then it should be abolished.
– Rediscover the meaning of inter-church aid and Christian service; that is to say, enable each both to give and to receive. Hence the growing quest for mutual aid and real sharing, in which each partner has something important and essential to contribute to the joint enterprise.

In conclusion, the paper proposed the abolition of the project list, starting in 1976, because that list could not form the basis of the new relations between equal and responsible partners to which the churches aspired.

During the period between the 1968 Uppsala Assembly and that of Nairobi in 1975, three particularly important questions connected with the practice of inter-church aid dominated the debate.

During those years, the churches had assisted each other and worked together, and inter-church aid, as presently practised, could genuinely be considered a sign of the growing unity of the church and an anticipation of the conciliar community of the future. The inter-church aid process is not static; world dynamics and the world ecumenical fellowship fashion it into new tasks and challenges.

Several issues have surfaced; they have not been resolved, they are still debated and will continue to be debated in the 1980s.

1. The *call for a moratorium* on funds and personnel from the West to the third world. First heard in 1971, it challenged all patterns of aid and was addressed in particular to the churches which had become dependent on and captive of the flow of foreign resources to carry out most of their services and activities.

The issue is whether the receiving church, by cutting the umbilical cord with outside churches, is liberated to create ties with sister churches within its own country and to build up links with the local population.

Inter-church aid has extended to all parts of the world where the churches' efforts are part of the struggles of societies whose major concern is *not to restore something* which has been temporarily removed, but to *install a new order* through involvement in decolonization, development, social and economic justice, and liberation from oppressive national and/or international structures.

This call for the churches to pause and to reflect *in situ* rather than to accept the mushrooming of aid relationships conducted speedily because of the pressure of available resources that have to be shared is still a serious ecumenical agenda item. Although seemingly asleep at the present time, the moratorium debate will have to be pursued.

2. The *project approach* in the inter-church aid relationships, the discussion on project systems and the search for a viable alternative continues to be a permanent concern. There is sufficient evidence to affirm that at the time when the churches should relate as equal partners respecting each other's stewardship, the structure of aid through project requests and funding seems inadequate. It perpetuates patterns of power, domination and dependence which should disappear from the churches' praxis in a true community. I refer the reader to the series of CICARWS papers and documents on this subject: "Whither the Project System?" (1973); "From Projects to Country Programmes" (1975); "Do We Project Ourselves in Projects?" (1977).

Recognizing the matter of importance, the Nairobi Assembly and the WCC Central Committee in 1976 mandated CICARWS to explore new ways of sharing resources and to experiment in this field. As a result, several experiments have been initiated, particularly with "country programmes" as an evolving model of collective action. Such programmes call for the churches in a local or national setting to plan together, to establish their own priorities for mission and service activities, and to share their own resources with each other before receiving any assistance from outside. Similarly, the giving churches are encouraged to provide a united, flexible response to such programmes. It was hoped that this pattern would develop in various parts of the world and would effectively eliminate many of the divisive aspects of aid, and thereby promote greater joint action and unity.

3. The *political implications of aid*. As long as inter-church aid was understood as "churches helping churches", it was very normal, neutral, and readily acceptable. It was taken for granted that churches belonging to the same family should assist each other. But as inter-church aid became involved in social action, participation in peoples' struggles for their development and liberation, and as it sought to respond to the cry for justice and not charity, it suddenly took on a controversial character. Humanitarian and solidarity efforts are not free from political aspects.

Perhaps the churches' involvement in the Nigeria-Biafra war (1968–69) demonstrated most clearly how inter-church aid practised by and with churches which are themselves in the midst of struggles, ceases to be a neutral act. Practice shows that inevitably choices have to be made.

The service efforts of the churches during the war in Vietnam, inter-church aid efforts with the churches in Chile and other Latin American countries to protect victims of human rights violations and refugees, solidarity with the racially oppressed in Southern Africa, are but a few examples of the complexity of the political issues that are intertwined with the churches' service and inter-church aid efforts. The churches active in such situations and ministering to the peoples involved, as well as those churches outside the situation which consider it important to speak out and deal with the root causes of the problems, are often criticized, threatened, silenced, and sometimes blackmailed by those in their midst who still dream of inter-church aid as a pure, neutral, or conscience-easing form of Christian service.

Obviously the debate over the Programme to Combat Racism shows that the move from helping victims of a situation to supporting those struggling to change their situation has become unacceptable to some people in some churches in some countries. The questions posed by such programmes, if faced seriously, can help us considerably to understand the contemporary meaning of inter-church aid and Christian service.

Since the Nairobi Assembly, various themes and subjects have dominated the research and thinking of CICARWS.

One of them, obviously, has been the ecumenical sharing of resources. The study has helped us to a deeper understanding of the fellowship constituted by the churches and various movements associated with the WCC and which they try to live out. Although several WCC Sub-units were involved, CICARWS bore responsibility for carrying into effect the conclusions of the study regarding the financing of projects and programmes of inter-church aid and exchange of personnel. As Philip Potter had occasion to say when opening one of the consultations convened in the course of that study:

> The issues raised by ecumenical sharing of resources are not new. . . We have been debating them for a very long time, but we have made scarcely any progress in practice. . . We must seek means of breaking the frustrating circle of repeated declarations which are received and filed, but not followed by any decision. . . We are "members of one another" and if that reality is not expressed by sharing, by relations of equality, solidarity and joint action, we are unfaithful to our vocation as members of the body of Christ.

In 1980 a "Message to the Churches" was adopted by the Central Committee and a study guide was published entitled *Empty Hands*. One phrase sums up perhaps the essence of this quest for genuine sharing: "sharing of what the churches are, not only what they have", and this was taken up again in other terms in the "Message to the Churches".

> "Do not be conformed to this world, but be transformed by the renewal of your mind" (Rom. 12:2). What will be the shape of a worldwide Church transformed in its pattern of sharing according to the values of the kingdom of God? We are only beginning to discover God's intent for us in this regard. Yet we have certain intimations of what that shape will be:
> – It will be a Church which affirms the mutual interdependence of all its parts, as each enters into the lives and needs of all the others, sharing their rejoicing and their suffering.
> – It will be a Church which rises above its various national identities and gratefully affirms its universality in Christ, employing the richness of its God-given resources to engage those basic problems confronting humankind.
> – It will be a Church in which decision-making is shared across the

world's divisions, and decision-making centres are diversified, from the level of the parish to the highest councils.
- It will be a Church which dares to confront the powers of this world, be they political, economic or cultural, and in the name of the crucified Christ call for justice for the poor and oppressed.

The manner in which the Church in Christ's name is willing to share, yes, to risk its resources, by God's grace, can be a parable for global sharing. In a world in which the language of faith has lost meaning for lack of translation into life, the acting out of God's kind of sharing announces as no words can the good news of Christ to humankind.

★   ★   ★

Luke's gospel captures the irony of the disciples disputing over who was greatest, immediately after Jesus had broken bread and given it to them saying: "This is my body." To the Church living in the midst of a power-hungry world, today Jesus says:
"Do this" – be broken for the world.[1]

Another equally important CICARWS concern has been that of *unity* and of the relation between *service and unity*, a topic which formed the subject of the meeting of the Commission in Strasbourg in July 1978, one year after my appointment as its director.

For my first programme report to the Commission, I had chosen the theme "Be doers of the word, and not hearers only" (James 1:22).

Our faith and our theological understanding makes us believe that we have a permanent obligation to serve, with courage and joy. Our service should not be weakened by pessimism and despair, our service, to be relevant, must aim at the elimination of the causes of misery, oppression and injustice.

Our analyses of the causes are becoming sharper and we know that complicated structures of injustice and oppression are maintained by powers and principalities that are strong but not invincible. . . .

In the ecumenical movement, one often heard it said that doctrine divides but service unites. That is perhaps less evident today than in the past, and some people go as far as to maintain, on the contrary, that doctrine unites but service divides. Our activity in the course of the last twenty years has shown us that:

Service, diakonia and the eucharist belong together, by sharing through bread and wine Christ's body, we become his body, we are made into share-people, are empowered to share with others our own lives, our gifts. Service, diakonia without thanksgiving has little

---

[1] *Empty Hands*, Geneva, WCC, 1980, pp. 7–8.

relationship to Christ: a eucharistic celebration without real commitment to serve the world in Christ's name is a pious act.

Service, with the inevitable political implications it carries in any attempt to work for greater justice, by uncovering the basic causes of injustice, will be divisive. If our understanding of confessing Christ means and implies taking sides, helping the oppressed to liberate themselves, tension will always inevitably be with us. This tension can only be creative if lived openly and honestly.

After full debate on the theme, the Commission adopted a statement declaring our convictions and relocating the vocation of service in the very centre of our Christian faith, unity in Jesus Christ and eucharistic fellowship.

> Unity is the work of the Holy Spirit and not the result of our own efforts, however ecumenical these may be. Service in obedience to the gospel will not unite nor divide more than Christ himself. . .
>
> . . . The experience of sharing has exposed the injustice and inequities in patterns of sharing within the household of faith and in the structures of society. The gospel continually forces us to grow beyond our prejudices and beyond the limitations of a comfortable fellowship. Preconceptions and conditions of sharing are challenged and rejected by those who seek to overcome patterns of dependence and domination. Our commitment to seek justice in relationships in the human family brings tensions and pain to our search for and experience of unity. . . .

In the following year 1979 we met again, in New Windsor (USA), to discuss the theme "Mutual Aid and Solidarity". I had been led to choose this topic and in particular that of solidarity, by the attitude of some colleagues who hesitated even to use the word because it was "loaded" and "coloured". We devoted the greater part of our time to an attempt to rediscover the meaning of the French word "entraide", which conveys so well the qualities of mutuality and reciprocity which define the nature of the relationship to which we aspired in our CICARWS network. To illustrate the meaning of our quest, I made use of a message of Philip Potter to the Central Committee on the text of St Paul: "Bear one another's burdens" (Gal. 6:2–5). The fulfilment of the "law of Christ", that is to say the whole substance of the Christian life, demands that we begin and continue to carry one another's burdens, and the word "burden" refers to the responsibilities which according to the apostle each of us must bear, but which become a burden when they are so heavy or so painful as to be intolerable, crushing, weakening our humanity and limiting our capacity to be fully ourselves.

This message well expresses the ideal we had in mind in defining and determining relations of partnership in inter-church aid.

Discussion of the word "solidarity" also enabled us to make clear the nature of the atmosphere and relationships which we wished to establish. For the word solidarity implies the quality of being profoundly united, together with the moral obligation not to be of disservice to others but to be of help to them, and also emphasizes the mutual dependence which means that it is impossible for some to be happy and develop while others do not.

Surely the word solidarity is pregnant with gospel values? To show that the concept could rightly be applied to our aspirations in the domain of inter-church aid and Christian service, I developed further the conditions of the "practice of solidarity".

– Entering into solidarity implies a commitment to change the structures which create the conditions of inferiority of the people with whom we wish to show our solidarity – a commitment, struggle, battle against injustice.

– To be in solidarity postulates the existence of partners with whom agreement is reached on goals to be achieved by joint concerted effort respectful of the identity of each.

– Practising solidarity means a continuing deep-rooted commitment, accomplishing concrete actions, accepting shared decision-making and by that very fact, giving it a prophetic political dimension in the sense that solidarity, if really lived out, can foreshadow the relations that ought to exist between countries, between communities, between groups and persons.

My last report presented at the meeting of the Commission in Yverdon in June 1981, took its inspiration from the theme of the Vancouver Assembly "Jesus Christ – the Life of the World". The previous year the Commission had met in Beirut, in devastated Lebanon, to deal with the theme "Servant Churches in a Divided World".

By considering the affirmation "Jesus Christ – the Life of the World", we wished to reflect on the basis of the activities of CICARWS, and rehabilitate diakonia, the "service of life" – our mandate.

> In proclaiming that Jesus Christ is the life of the world we affirm his Lordship and his coming kingdom; we affirm that his church and his disciples are sent into the world to give their lives; this is the service to which we are called.
>
> It may seem pretentious to state that *diakonia* is the service of life. Diakonia is a well-worn word, often it smacks of attitudes which have ceased to be relevant to the circumstances of life at the end of the twentieth century. Diakonia sounds rather old-fashioned and, like charity, perhaps a bit retrograde. So we must try to restore the true meaning to the word diakonia and rehabilitate diakonia as such. This

will call for service which is imaginative, bold and, consequently, prophetic.

It is generally held that the institution of diakonia (Acts 6), with the appointment of the first seven deacons, was intended to relieve the apostles of material tasks and leave them free to devote themselves to the preaching of the word. However, at the very beginning of the affair there was an injustice, an instance of discrimination: ". . . widows were being overlooked in the daily distribution". It was to redress this injustice that a number of Hellenists, members of an oppressed minority, were appointed to wait at table, as a measure to guard against injustice and marginalization.

When we look at our world and see all the men and women who are constantly overlooked in the daily distribution. . . Our diakonia must aim to re-establish justice, not to distribute the left-overs to those who are neglected, discriminated against, marginalized.

To do this, our diaconal service must actively oppose the forces which are seeking to destroy life; it cannot make do with bringing solace and aid to people who have already been struck down and broken by those forces. Its role is preventive as much as curative.

Diakonia cannot be "reasonable" or "respectable". It is throwing down a challenge to those life-destroying forces, to the "powers", not least those of money and possession. In a world where everything is counted, where everything can be bought and sold, where ownership is everything, diakonia seeks to set a sign of great freedom: giving everything freely, asking nothing in return, doing so out of love and gratitude, as a sign of joyful sacrifice, living, holy and acceptable. This is not reasonable! Diakonia is not reasonable from the point of view of the captains of industry, or advertising strategies or the guardians of the absolute given values of work, order, ownership, national security, and so on. Diakonia is out of step with the modern world. It asks each and everyone freely to give him or herself for a new world.

Anyone who loves or has ever loved knows full well that if reason were the only thing that counted. . .

Anyone who has shared his or her goods and life joyfully, expecting nothing in return, knows that if reason were the only thing that counted. . .

Anyone who wants to follow the risen Christ knows full well that the resurrection is not reasonable. . .

This understanding of diakonia lets us situate our action in relation to the overall effort of the World Council of Churches, its Unit on Justice and Service and the action of the churches. A total service, intended for the whole of humanity, affirming the forces of life.

The Diaconal Task of the Churches Today

Statement approved by WCC Central Committee, Geneva, July 1984

The Central Committee notes that 1984 marks the fortieth anniversary of the founding of what is now the Commission on Inter-Church Aid, Refugee and World Service (CICARWS). It is a significant fact that even before the official founding of the WCC in 1948, and within the agonizing years of the Second World War, the churches needed and created this instrument for the expression of their growing sense of the universal koinonia of the church of Jesus Christ, and for a practical demonstration that when one suffers, all suffer.

As the Vancouver Assembly stated "the church exists in the midst of the world where brokenness and lack of harmony find their expression not only in sickness and conflicts, but also in the marginalization and oppression that many people endure due to economic, racial, political, cultural and often religious reasons. This situation is a challenge to the Church to carry out its healing ministry in a holistic way, renewed by the power of Christ's love which is the basis of the ministry" (Issue IV: Healing and Sharing Life in Community).

"The Church as the living body of Christ, by its very nature and mission, is a *koinonia* (communion) of sharing and healing. . . As we share in Christ's broken body, so we become bread for the world to *be* broken. This implies cross, *kenosis* (self-emptying), which disturbs us creatively" (Issue IV). It also implies discipleship and sacrifice in Christian diaconal work for social justice and human dignity.

Our understanding of the causes of human suffering, our ways and means of preventing and alleviating human need, our awareness of the inter-relatedness and interdependence of all people, and the obligation of Christians to demonstrate that awareness have all grown through experience. Even while recognizing our failures, we give thanks to God for the churches' work and witness, which has assisted millions of needy people over four decades.

It is impossible to mention the many church initiatives that have been taken during the forty past years. But we do give thanks in recalling, for example, the provision of temporary churches for many of Europe's bombed cities, the services to millions of persons displaced by the Second World War, the expansion into a six continent response to desperate human need, the tangible presence of the church in hundreds of disaster situations, the ministry to the suffering on both sides of armed conflicts, the refugee service and resettlement, rehabilitation and reconstruction programmes on every continent, the care for migrants, the provision of thousands of scholarships, and the participation in tens of thousands of service and development projects of local churches. All these activities were tangible expressions of ecumenical solidarity and helped the building-up of trust and fellowship among churches all over the world.

These multi-faceted activities have been undergirded by a continuous process of study and reflection on the meaning of the diaconal task of CICARWS, its theological rationale, its role in promoting social justice and human development, its understanding of what ecumenical sharing of resources is all about, its impact on the churches' search for unity and community.

"Diakonia as the church's ministry of sharing, healing and reconciliation is of the very nature of the church. It demands of individuals and churches a giving which comes not out of what they have, but what they are. Diakonia constantly has to challenge the frozen, static, self-centred structures of the church and transform them into living instruments of the sharing and healing ministry of the church. Diakonia cannot be confined within the institutional framework. It should transcend the established structures and boundaries of the institutional church and become the sharing and healing action of the Holy Spirit through the community of God's people in and for the world" (Issue IV). The Vancouver Assembly, considering the diaconal role of the church, challenged its member churches and CICARWS to revise and revitalize their efforts in the field of diakonia and to ensure that their efforts are closely related to the wider quest for peace, justice and the integrity of creation.

We are profoundly thankful for the continued existence and action of the Commission within the wider fellowship of the Programme Unit on Justice and Service of the World Council of Churches, and we assure the Commission members, director and staff of our prayers, as we have done for their predecessors over the years. But above all we remember with thankfulness the churches and their agencies around the world, in both the richer and poorer lands, which have been primary actors in all that has been attempted.

The United Nations
High Commissioner for Refugees

A Tribute to Cooperation

The fortieth anniversary of the Commission on Inter-Church Aid, Refugee and World Service is a fitting occasion for UNHCR to review the close cooperation that has existed between the two organizations and also to look forward towards the future.

CICARWS' involvement in refugee work dates back to the post-Second World War period, when the United Nations Relief and Rehabilitation Administration (UNRRA) and later the International Refugee Organization (IRO) assisted displaced persons in Europe. When the Office of the United Nations High Commissioner for Refugees (UNHCR) was created in 1951, CICARWS became one of UNHCR's first operational partners. Since that time CICARWS has maintained a close relationship with the Office, working as UNHCR's partner in refugee programmes around the world. CICARWS acts either directly or indirectly, through national or local churches or through ecumenical agencies. CICARWS is thus one of UNHCR's longest-standing partners both in operational terms and in terms of consultation and dialogue on refugee issues.

Since UNHCR is not operational, in accordance with the terms of its mandate, cooperation with non-governmental organizations (NGOs) has always been an integral feature of the High Commissioner's programmes. Indeed, the Statute of the Office makes specific reference to assisting private organizations in promoting voluntary repatriation or assimilation of refugees into new communities, subject to the approval of the governments concerned.

The first and foremost role of UNHCR is the international protection of refugees with which the Office has been specifically entrusted by the United Nations General Assembly. In carrying out this task, UNHCR strives to ensure that refugees are protected against *refoulement*, that they be granted asylum and that their rights be recognized by asylum countries.

Traditionally, the churches have been involved in providing material assistance to refugees. Today, however, along with certain other non-governmental organizations, the churches are playing an increasing role in the field of international protection. The churches not only call UNHCR's attention to cases of violation of refugee rights, but have also, for example, provided a permanent presence at airports in Europe in order to deal with restrictive asylum procedures and questions of *refoulement*. The churches' deep concern with questions of international protection and asylum issues has resulted in a number of meetings, some of which have been attended by UNHCR, such as the important meetings held in 1984 on assistance to asylum seekers at international airports and protection of asylum seekers in Western countries.

The system of law dealing with international refugee protection is constantly being developed and refined. There exists, for example, an ongoing discussion regarding the refugee definition which was first set out in the Statute of the Office of the United Nations High Commissioner for Refugees and in the United Nations Convention of 1951 relating to the Status of Refugees. In accordance with these instruments, a refugee is a victim of persecution due to reasons of race, religion, nationality, political opinion or membership of a social group.

However, in the context of the political reality which has evolved during the last three decades, it became evident that large numbers of persons were compelled to leave their home countries, not for any specific fear of persecution, but in order to seek protection from danger due to serious internal upheavals or armed conflicts. In recognizing that such persons are also of concern to the international community, the General Assembly, through various resolutions, has given the high commissioner the competence to concern himself with these persons who are sometimes referred to as displaced persons in a refugee-like situation. Besides, the secretary-general may also ask the high commissioner to use his good offices in specific situations. The Office has thus been in a position to concern itself with affected populations in Lebanon and in Cyprus.

Furthermore, on the African continent, following the endorsement through a General Assembly resolution of the Arusha recommendation on the definition of the term "refugee" in Africa, UNHCR is mandated to apply the broader definition which is included in the 1969 OAU Convention governing the specific aspects of refugee problems in Africa. The churches, however, have consistently adopted an even broader approach to the refugee definition, which includes internally displaced persons as well as those who suffer persecution for reasons not specified in the Statute or in the 1951 UN Convention. This wider interpretation held by the churches gives them the scope to intervene in specific situations which are beyond UNHCR's mandate.

Another refugee-related area in which the churches have played a leading role is that of examining root causes of refugee flows. UNHCR, because of its mandate, is not in a position to concern itself with root causes. In recent years, however, this issue has been studied by numerous non-governmental organizations, predominantly church groups, which have succeeded in attracting international attention to the various "push-pull factors" behind refugee movements.

In view of the rapidly changing refugee situations around the world, it has been particularly beneficial for UNHCR to be able to rely on its cooperation with the church network. In many cases, it is the churches which are closest both to the populations of asylum countries and to the refugee populations themselves. This grassroots level contact enables the churches to provide highly effective and humanitarian services in areas such as counselling and to facilitate all aspects of refugee integration. Church groups in countries of asylum are also often familiar with legislation affecting refugee status as well as with social benefits available to refugees, including education, housing and employment. The churches are thus well-suited to accompany the refugee through the various phases of his/her exodus, to a degree which cannot be matched in the same way by an international organization such as UNHCR.

UNHCR cooperation with the churches has been particularly strong in Africa where the All Africa Conference of Churches (AACC), a regional counterpart of the World Council of Churches, is one of UNHCR's major partners. In certain countries in Africa UNHCR works through the national Christian councils whose member churches belong to the AACC and the WCC. The churches' major areas of refugee service in Africa include urban counselling, education and training, as well as material assistance. In Kenya, for example, the National Council of Churches provides refugees with counselling, scholarships and general assistance, while the Church of the Province of Kenya provides emergency aid to refugees not assisted by UNHCR. The churches provide similar services in Djibouti, Tanzania, Zambia, Swaziland, Botswana, Zimbabwe, Senegal, Zaire, Rwanda and Burundi. In Ethiopia UNHCR is about to start a counselling project for urban refugees with the Ethiopian Orthodox Church.

Since the beginning of the Indochinese refugee crisis, the churches have worked together with UNHCR in providing needed services to refugees in Thailand. The Church of Christ in Thailand, for example, works with Hmong, Lao and Vietnamese refugees in the camps of Ban Vinai, Ha Pho and Sikhiu, providing social assistance and health care.

The churches have also demonstrated their solidarity with the Afghan refugees who now number almost three million in Pakistan. The Inter-Aid Committee of Karachi, which brings together both Protestant and Catholic churches, works with refugees in Baluchistan and the North West Frontier Province providing them with medical assistance, education and relief supplies.

In Latin America the churches have traditionally played an important role in the social and cultural fabric of the different societies and, as such, are welcome partners in UNHCR programmes in Argentina, Brazil, Chile and Costa Rica. In Chile, for example, the Fundación de Ayuda Social de las Iglesias Cristianas (Foundation for Social Work of the Christian Churches) has provided a wide variety of services to refugees and returnees, including family reunification, material assistance to returnees and, when necessary, resettlement facilities.

In Costa Rica the church agencies have also played a most important role in the refugee field. The Episcopal Church of Costa Rica was UNHCR's first operational partner in that country providing assistance to individual cases. More recently, the Episcopal Church of Costa Rica has set up its own programme of social services for refugees, particularly those suffering from psychological trauma, and has created self-reliance projects in the form of cooperatives. Furthermore the Comité Ecuménico por Derechos Humanos (Ecumenical Human Rights' Committee) makes available legal services to refugees in Costa Rica.

In the past UNHCR agreements with local church agencies were signed at the Geneva level by the World Council of Churches. Now, in accordance with the World Council's decentralization policy, UNHCR maintains direct links with local churches and signs agreements, wherever possible, at the field level.

The churches have also demonstrated their willingness to work together with UNHCR by seconding staff to UNHCR programmes. In Singapore, Somalia and Senegal, WCC staff have worked in UNHCR refugee assistance programmes, particularly in the area of social services. In Central America volunteers from different church groups have helped to provide an international presence in several refugee camps.

Many members of the worldwide network of the ecumenical family provide strong, tangible support to UNHCR's refugee assistance programmes. A number of church agencies, particularly those in Europe, have traditionally contributed both in cash and kind to UNHCR programmes and appeals.

In terms of reflection on refugee issues, the relationship between UNHCR and the World Council of Churches is mutually reinforcing. UNHCR welcomes participation by church agencies in UNHCR/NGO meetings and in sessions of the Consultative Group on International Protection. The advocacy role played by the churches vis-à-vis governments and public opinion is an important support to UNHCR's efforts in favour of more liberal policies towards refugees.

The objectives set by the World Council of Churches include not only to provide material assistance to refugees, but also to assist in the struggle for a more just world characterized by fewer refugees. Motivated by this goal, which is fully shared by UNHCR, CICARWS has played a key role in providing valuable services to refugees. At this time, when refugee situations are growing both in number and complexity, UNHCR and CICARWS need to cooperate more closely than ever before. While both the Office and the churches have their own priorities and prerogatives, their work is highly complementary and together they can provide a comprehensive response to refugee needs. UNHCR looks forward to continuing and strengthening its partnership with CICARWS in the spirit of the objectives set forward by the World Council of Churches.

Directors

W. A. Visser 't Hooft	to April 1945
J. Hutchison Cockburn	April 1945–December 1948
Robert C. Mackie	January 1949–Summer 1955
Leslie E. Cooke	Summer 1955–February 1967
Charles W. Arbuthnot (acting)	February 1967–March 1968
Charlotte Browne-Mayers	April 1968–July 1969
Jan Ørner (acting)	August 1969–March 1970
Alan A. Brash	April 1970–December 1973
Graeme C. Jackson (acting)	January–September 1974
Muriel S. Webb	October 1974–July 1977
Jean E. Fischer	August 1977–July 1982
Georges Tsetsis (acting)	August–December 1982
Nicholas J. Maro	January 1983–December 1984

Contributors

SAMUEL H. AMISSAH (Ghana)
was general secretary of the All Africa Conference of Churches 1964–71.

ARCHBISHOP ATHANASIOS (Egypt)
for many years spiritual father of one of the biggest dioceses of Egypt, was until recently responsible for the Coptic Orthodox Church's Bishopric of Public, Ecumenical and Social Services.

ALAN A. BRASH (New Zealand)
served the East Asian Christian Conference and Christian Aid/ UK, was director of CICARWS 1970–73 and later deputy general secretary of the WCC.

ULRICH VON BRÜCK (German Democratic Republic)
was director of the Inner Mission and Relief Agency of the Evangelical Lutheran Church of Saxony 1950–59 and of Bread for the World/GDR 1959–80.

JEAN E. FISCHER (Switzerland)
after missionary service in Northern Rhodesia (now Zambia), joined CICARWS in 1964 and was its director 1977–82.

MARTA PALMA (Chile)
of the Pentecostal Mission Church has been a member of the CICARWS Commission since 1976.

ALEXANDROS PAPADEROS (Greece)
a lay theologian of the Church of Crete (Orthodox), has been director of the Orthodox Academy in Crete since 1967.

KATHLEEN PTOLEMY (Canada)
formerly served the Canadian Interchurch Committee for Refugees, and now works with the Anglican Church of Canada.

KENNETH SLACK (UK)
was general secretary of the British Council of Churches 1955–65 and director of Christian Aid in that Council 1975–82.

KYAW THAN (Burma)
was associated with the East Asia Christian Conference since its inception, and its general secretary until 1973.

HANS THIMME (Federal Republic of Germany)
past president of the Evangelical Church in Germany, was moderator of CICARWS 1969–75.

UNITED NATIONS HIGH COMMISSIONER FOR REFUGEES
Liaison Unit with Non-Governmental Organizations
WILLEM A. VISSER 'T HOOFT (Netherlands)
was general secretary of the World Council of Churches 1948–66
and later its honorary president.